Stephenson | *Mrs Thatcher's first year*

Hugh Stephenson was born in India in 1938. He was educated at Winchester and New College, Oxford, where he was President of the Union. After two years as a Commonwealth Fund Fellow at the University of California, he entered the Diplomatic Service. In 1968 he joined *The Times* and has been the editor of its Business News since 1971. In 1972 he published his first book, *The Coming Clash*, a study of international companies and their impact on nation states.

D0715524

MRS THATCHER'S FIRST YEAR

HUGH STEPHENSON

JILL NORMAN

Jill Norman Ltd
90 Great Russell Street, London WC1 3PY

First published 1980
© Hugh Stephenson 1980

Printed in Great Britain
by The Anchor Press Ltd
and bound by
Wm Brendon and Son Ltd

British Library Cataloguing in Publication Data

Stephenson, Hugh
    Mrs Thatcher's first year.
    1. Great Britain – Politics and government – 1964 –
    I. Title

    941.085'7   DA592

ISBN 0–906908–16–7
ISBN 0–906908–05–1 Pbk

Contents

Acknowledgements

I AM DEEPLY INDEBTED to all those who gave so freely of their time to give me their impressions of Mrs Thatcher and her government in its first year. I hope that I have not abused any confidences.

My family are owed an equal debt for their tolerance while the book was being written.

Introduction

MRS THATCHER WAS GIVEN A free piece of advice before she became Prime Minister. It came from a friend and adviser, the chairman of a major public company. He told her that she should not do anything rash in her first hundred days that she might later regret. But, as she went into No. 10 Downing Street that Friday, 4 May, as the first woman Prime Minister of the United Kingdom, Mrs Thatcher was also pulled in the other direction. She knew that there is no moment when an incoming government's freedom of manoeuvre is greater than at the very beginning, riding high upon a massive victory at the polls.

She had drawn a lesson from her experience in the 1970-74 Heath government. Unless action is taken to change policy in the first few months, it rapidly becomes impossible to make any change at all. Our system of government has an inbuilt tendency to preserve the status quo and to find strong arguments against change. Margaret Thatcher knew that she at least was coming to office with a clear personal vision of a crusading kind. She expressed it two days before the election, speaking in Bolton, when she said, 'Unless we change our ways and our direction, our greatness as a nation will soon be a footnote in the history books, a distant memory of an off-shore island lost in the mists of time – like Camelot remembered kindly for its noble past.' In that vision, the country under her leadership was going to turn aside from the low road, or dead-end, of post-war consensus politics and take instead a new and untried high road out of the Slough of Despond. But an evangelist preaching a new and radical message to a still largely reluctant and uncomprehending congregation dare not talk the language of realism and political compromise at the start of the journey. Revolutions require momentum.

Other factors were also pulling her in different directions. On the face of it, her authority was unquestionable. She had led her party to victory in what she called in her first speech as Prime Minister to the House of Commons 'a watershed election. The result was decisive, with a difference of two million votes between the two major parties, the largest difference since 1935.' The margin in the popular vote, indeed, was greater than in the Labour landslide victory of 1945, or Harold Macmillan's post-Suez Conservative triumph in 1959. The election had brought to an end a period of more than five years during which the government of the day was a minority, coalition government, or had only the barest majority in the House of commons. Now the Conservatives had a majority of 44 seats over all the opposition parties combined. Such a majority meant that the government was safe for the full five years of a parliament, barring only a major revolt amongst its own back-benchers.

Against that, however, Mrs Thatcher had certain potential and important weaknesses in her position. First, she was a woman. This had certainly proved no disadvantage, probably on balance an advantage, so far as winning the election had been concerned. But how would she handle the still almost wholly masculine world of government itself? Secondly, though her election and pre-election strategy had been triumphantly vindicated on polling day, this did not alter the fact that in vital areas of policy she did not have the support of the majority of her senior parliamentary colleagues.

More importantly, she came to No. 10 as the least experienced Prime Minister in modern times. In fact she had only ever had two government posts. From 1961 to 1964, she had been Joint Parliamentary Secretary to the Ministry of Pensions and National Insurance, neither a post nor a ministry which gave any experience of the main levers of political power. Her only Cabinet experience was her three and a half years as the statutory woman in Mr Heath's 1970–74 government, when she was Minister of Education. Compared with the length and breadth of experience of previous Prime Ministers in the major departments of state, like the Treasury and the Foreign Office, she was remarkably untrained for the job.

The juxtaposition of these strengths and weaknesses, personal and political, which Mrs Thatcher brought to Downing Street, created the tensions that determined the character of her first year as Prime Minister. In a sense, a year is an artificial period over which to study a Prime Minister or a government. But in this case enough has happened within that first year to indicate clearly the direction in which the 'Thatcher Experiment' is going. Her government has had two budgets. There has been time to observe the reactions to 'Thatcherism' of the Cabinet, the wider Conservative party, the Civil Service and the nation as a whole.

There are, of course, severe difficulties about writing when we are still so close to the events. A book, by its very nature, makes a claim to be something more than instant journalism. Yet it is clearly impossible to make lasting historical judgments. No documents are available. No diaries have been written, let alone published. The memory of those who have participated in events and are prepared to talk about them may be clear, but they are still too close to them to be able to see them in any perspective. So I make no excessive claims that this book has discovered great and lasting truths about Mrs Thatcher or her government. The evidence has of necessity been too anecdotal in character for that. There may also be more errors of fact than there should be in a serious work, because of the speed with which it has been produced.

Nor has my purpose been to produce a full chronicle of the events of the twelve months from May 1979. It has been to capture the perceptions of people close to those events, so that they may be available to those who later wish to recall how it seemed at the time. My method has been to talk to a wide cross-section of people directly and indirectly involved in the impact of Mrs Thatcher and her government on public life. In distilling this evidence I am aware of the danger that all judgments are subjective. However, there is one conclusion about Margaret Thatcher for which there is sufficient evidence to allow of some confidence. It is that she carries within herself a permanent conflict between the reactions of the political visionary and the reactions of the gut politician. It makes her a much more complex and often contradictory figure than appears on the surface. Her rhetoric is radical, even reckless. But from the start her deeds have shown a politician's instinctive caution.

April 1980

Chapter 1

Time for a new beginning

Where there is discord, may we bring harmony.
Where there is error, may we bring truth.
Where there is doubt, may we bring faith.
Where there is despair, may we bring hope.

Mrs Thatcher, quoting St Francis of Assisi, as she entered No. 10 Downing St as Prime Minister.

IN OUR CURIOUS UNWRITTEN CONSTITUTION the Prime Minister has a uniquely powerful position. The power stems from the patronage that is at the Prime Minister's disposal. And it is at its most absolute at the start of a new government, before the first Cabinet colleague has been offered and has accepted a job. For, from the moment the major Cabinet appointments have been made, a Prime Minister has at least to begin to take into account the views and feelings of others. Much interest, therefore, centred on how Mrs Thatcher would use her power in giving her first administration its shape.

The basic question was to what extent she would prefer the overt supporters of her brand of Toryism and those who had organised her coup against Heath for the leadership of the party in 1975. To what extent would she use her freedom to correct the fact that, as Leader of the Opposition, her Shadow Cabinet had been predominantly made up of the men who had worked closely with Heath? To what extent would she promote to senior positions people whose instincts were closer to her own on economic policy, trade unions, Rhodesia, immigration, hanging, or law and order?

Her choice in practice was circumscribed by the fact that she had failed to follow a private piece of advice, given to her some 18 months earlier by the executive of the 1922 Committee, the body representing all back-bench Conservative members of the House of Commons.

It had been an unusual episode, reflecting a feeling that the party had found itself being led by someone short of practical political experience. Senior Tory back-benchers and the chairman of the 1922

Committee, Edward Du Cann, thought it would be a good thing if Mrs Thatcher made a re-shuffle of her main Shadow Cabinet posts long before any prospective general election. The argument went that she would then have much greater freedom of manoeuvre when she came to pick her first actual Cabinet, because there would be a range of senior figures with at least 'shadow' experience of more than one portfolio. The executive's feelings on this subject were so strong that it formally gave the Leader advice to this effect.

Mrs Thatcher toyed with the idea. She was not convinced, for example, that the Shadow Chancellor, Sir Geoffrey Howe, would make a sufficiently robust Chancellor. She is said to have half hoped for a while that someone else would also emerge with the ideas and stature necessary for this critical job. In some ways she must have wished that her tutor and mentor in economic affairs, Sir Keith Joseph, could have taken on the role. But she knew that he lacked the physical and emotional stability required for what is always the most demanding job in any government . In the event, she had no major shake-up at the top and so went into the 1979 general election with substantially the same senior team that she had inherited when she became Leader.

Mrs Thatcher produced, as a result, a Cabinet almost entirely devoid of major surprises, most of the portfolios going to those who had held them in Opposition. Unusually for an incoming Prime Minister, she dealt personally not only with the senior appointments, but with the great majority of the others as well. If there was a surprise, it was that she went out of her way to stress continuity and caution by offering Cabinet posts to two of the party's elder statesmen, Lord Hailsham, aged 71, as Lord Chancellor, and Angus Maude, aged 66, as Paymaster General with responsibility for projecting the government's message.

It was almost as if the outsider, who against the odds had toppled Edward Heath to become leader of the Conservative party and then the country's first woman Prime Minister at the age of 53, was being careful not to lose the endorsement and support of the party establishment. Not for the first time, people noticed the way in which Mrs Thatcher drew advice and a sense of security from the company of men older than herself. In her campaign for the leadership and in the years before the election her office was run by Airey Neave, who was 63 when murdered by the IRA. In Opposition she developed an exceptionally close relationship with the chairman of the party, Lord Thorneycroft, aged almost 69 by the time of the election, as well as with Angus Maude, the deputy chairman.

Mrs Thatcher knew, though, from her period as Leader of the Opposition that her central policies would be still-born unless she had a core of ministers in key positions who shared her convictions. She knew that many of the radical attitudes and policies which she had presented in her election campaign had become election commitments despite the majority of her Shadow Cabinet and not because of them. So she put a small group of like-minded colleagues in key positions concerned with government spending, taxation, economic policy and the reduction of government involvement in industry. Her appointments in these areas were a clear indication of where she wanted to concentrate her attention.

The most senior of these appointments was that of Sir Keith Joseph to the Department of Industry. In the period since the Heath government lost power in 1974, Joseph had become, with all the fervour of a late convert, the arch proponent of the doctrine that the state should intervene as little as possible in the economy; and that the greatest public good derives from private individuals and companies pursuing their own interests. To put Joseph in charge of the one Whitehall department whose whole purpose was to pursue active government industrial policies was the political equivalent of putting a monk in charge of a whore-house.

Her key appointment at the Treasury was John Biffen as Chief Secretary. At an earlier stage Biffen might have emerged as a possible candidate for the chancellorship itself, in place of Howe. But in 1977 he had found the strain of front-bench responsibilities as chief Opposition spokesman on energy and industry too much and had returned to the back benches. By adding him to the existing Treasury team as Howe's number two, directly concerned with public expenditure, and by making him the second Treasury minister with a seat in the Cabinet, she was putting a supporter in a key position. The same applied to her appointment of John Nott to the Department of Trade and, to a lesser extent, to her giving the Department of Energy to David Howell, instead of to the previous energy spokesman, Tom King.

For the rest, the make-up of the Cabinet and government could only be described as extremely conventional and cautious. There was some speculation that she might offer a senior job, even perhaps at the Treasury, to Edward Du Cann, the long serving chairman of the 1922 Committee. He is a prominent City figure, if a controversial one as a director of Lonrho (the international trading company that caused Ted Heath to coin the phrase 'the unacceptable face of capitalism'), and as the former chairman of Keyser Ullmann (a secondary bank which got into serious trouble during the financial crisis of 1974). She certainly owed him a double debt of political gratitude. First, as chairman of the 1922 Committee, he had played a prominent role in the moves to oust Heath as leader after his second 1974 election defeat. And, secondly, he had done much from the same position to ensure that she had as smooth a relationship as possible with the parliamentary party once she became Leader. In any event, she went at least to the trouble of sending him a message to the effect that, on getting to No. 10, she had been shown a report into an unsavoury take-over six years earlier of a company called Grendon Trust by Christopher Selmes, a fast-moving fringe City figure. That report, due to be published within a matter of days, contained severe criticisms of the conduct of Keyser Ullmann and of Du Cann, who had been bankers and advisers to Selmes. She therefore hoped he would understand that she felt unable to offer him a job.

By the time of the election there was never any question of Mrs Thatcher offering Heath a job. There had been various attempts in the previous three years to arrange a reconciliation between them by those who thought that Heath's talents, energy and experience were being wasted. A mixture of his bitter inability to forgive what he saw as her act of disloyalty in standing against him for the leadership and her own uncertainty about her standing and authority doomed all such mediation to failure. Still, feelers were put out to him in good faith to see whether he was interested in any of a list of non-Cabinet jobs. He was offered, for example, the ambassadorship to the United States. He was also asked whether he would be interested in being a candidate for a number of international jobs with independent status, where he would not be responsible to ministers who had previously served under him; for example, as Secretary-General to NATO, or President of the EEC Commission, or at the World Bank in Washington. He turned down all these private approaches with what seemed a lack of grace, giving the impression that he would almost have preferred the Conservatives to have lost the election; for in that case the party would almost certainly have dumped Mrs Thatcher as Leader and might have turned back to him.

For the rest, Mrs Thatcher played safe, making no appointments that would upset the centre and left of her party. Francis Pym, as Shadow Foreign Secretary, wanted the Foreign and Commonwealth Office. But so, too, did Lord Carrington. As Leader of the Conservatives in the House of Lords he had carried a considerable burden on her behalf, particularly in establishing for her a working relationship with those sections of the party in the Upper House which had not been in favour of having her as Leader. So Lord Carrington went to the Foreign Office and Pym had to settle for Defence.

In giving Jim Prior the Department of Employment and Mark Carlisle the education portfolio, she took into her Cabinet two ministers distinctly out of sympathy with the views of right-wing Conservatives about their special areas. Indeed, though Prior at least was more or less happy with what the election manifesto had said on the subject of trade union reform, Carlisle was known to be distinctly unenthusiastic about the only specific manifesto commitment on education, the introduction of the 'assisted places scheme', designed to enable less well-off parents to claim all or part of the fees at certain private schools from a special new government fund. In the case of Jim Prior, Mrs Thatcher's political motives were at least clear. He had a substantial base within the party.

The appointment of Mark Carlisle was, however, a much clearer indication of her unwillingness to make radical experiments. Carlisle is an unassuming barrister apparently without strong political ambitions. He had been a junior minister at the Home Office in the Heath government. When he was invited by Mrs Thatcher in 1978 to become her front-bench spokesman on education he was hesitant. He had no particular knowledge of the subject and she made it absolutely clear to him that the shadow appointment carried no promise whatsoever that he would get the actual job in any future Cabinet. Since being the Opposition spokesman would involve a considerable reduction in his earnings from the Bar, it was only with some reluctance that he eventually accepted.

In the short period that he served as shadow education spokesman, Carlisle worked quietly to dilute the impact of the radical right on the party's education policy, which his predecessor Norman

St John-Stevas had rather encouraged. There was, therefore, every reason why Mrs Thatcher should choose instead of him an education minister closer to her own instinctive feelings.

In the event, not only did she take Carlisle into her Cabinet, but she allowed him effectively to muzzle Rhodes Boyson, the flamboyant, right-wing, ex-comprehensive school head master who had become something of a symbol of the radical backlash in education politics. He first entered Parliament in 1974 and became part of the Opposition's education team two years later. He was offered and accepted a job as a junior minister under Carlisle in the Department of Education on the clear assumption that he would be directly responsible for policy toward secondary schools. Senior officials in the department, knowing Boyson's views on secondary schools, feared that he would cause ructions just at a time when state secondary school reorganisation, which had been a political football since 1965, was beginning to settle down. They argued with Carlisle that Boyson should be given other responsibilities and found that the minister agreed. When Carlisle put this to the Prime Minister, he found, rather to his surprise, that instead of having to fight for his ground, he was told that it was his department and, therefore, up to him to decide how he organised it. So, to the fury of Boyson, a formula was devised whereby he was given responsibility for universities and higher education, while policy for schools was given to Carlisle's deputy, Lady Young, a personal friend of Mrs Thatcher, who had been given a life peerage in 1971 for her work as leader of the Conservatives on Oxford City Council. As a sop, since Lady Young sat in the House of Lords, Boyson was allowed to deputise for her on schools in the House of Commons.

The only other distinctive feature of Mrs Thatcher's first government was that she gave jobs to a rather larger number of peers than most people had expected. This was odd only for the fact that, since the Conservatives had only been out of office for just over five years, Mrs Thatcher was faced with an unusual number of experienced MPs, willing and able to be junior ministers.

These included people like Terence Higgins, Kenneth Baker, David Madel, John Biggs-Davison and Winston Churchill. Higgins had been at the Treasury in the previous government, but had decidedly liberal views on Rhodesia and immigration. Baker had been at the Civil Service Department, but had been Heath's Parliamentary

Private Secretary for a brief period during 1974. Madel was a vice-chairman of the party's employment committee and had been in the House since 1970. Biggs-Davison, though somewhat eccentric, had been a front-bench spokesman on Northern Ireland for four years, until he defied the Whips by voting against the renewal of Rhodesian sanctions in 1978 and had resigned. Churchill had been fired as an Opposition spokesman on defence for the same reason. His omission from the government, however, which some thought unimaginative at the time, stemmed more from his poor relations with the outgoing Chief Whip, Humphrey Atkins, on whose advice Mrs Thatcher was relying heavily in making the lower appointments.

In the event, Margaret Thatcher's first government included no less than twelve peers with departmental responsibilities, ten of whom were either in the Cabinet or had the status of ministers. With a majority as large as the one she enjoyed, Mrs Thatcher had no pressing need to maximise the 'payroll' vote in the House of Commons, but in terms of using junior ministerial appointments to bring on and try out promising material for later promotion, it may have been a mistake.

So much for the team that Margaret Thatcher put together over that first week-end in May. Her more substantial and difficult task, however, was going to be to translate the aspirations of Opposition and the election campaign into the realities of politics. The prospects would have been daunting to anyone with a less strong will and without a conviction that will-power can alter the trend of events.

There were the obvious problems, as she was soon to discover, like the fact that the underlying trends in the economy were worse than had been expected. She knew, too, that she would be operating through a Civil Service machine which at best did not understand the central themes of the Thatcher crusade and at worse actively disagreed with them. More important, she would have to come to terms with the political folk memory of the 1970-74 Conservative government of which, of course, she had been a member.

Indeed, just as James Callaghan's first reaction to any situation when he became Prime Minister, seemed to be to ask himself how his predecessor would have handled the situation and then to do the opposite, so Mrs Thatcher seemed determined not to follow the Heath style and pattern. Thus, for example, she had refused to repeat the solid and methodical research into policies which the Conservatives had done before the 1970 election, orchestrated first by

Sir Edward Boyle and then by Reginald Maudling. By contrast, the Conservative manifesto of 1979 was long on general statements of principle about the need to redress the balance that 'had been increasingly tilted in favour of the state at the expense of individual freedom'. It was unusually short on specific commitments. This was a deliberate decision not to repeat what had come to be seen as the mistake of going into the 1970 election with a rigid and detailed programme that cracked under the realities of office.

But the problem of Mrs Thatcher's relationship with Heath went deeper. As the *Economist* put it in a pre-election profile of her on 21 April, 'The ghost of the Heath administration looms over all discussion of Mrs Thatcher's policy and style, and neither her colleagues nor her critics can take their eyes off it. Can she lay it to rest? Has she found the philosopher's stone of modern Toryism, turning the base metal of political ideology to the gold of prime ministerial success? Or is she doomed to discredit that ideology by turning against it, as Mr Heath did, in the heat of office?'

The question was a valid one. To a substantial extent the Conservative programme on which Heath won in 1970 was based on the same themes that dominated the 1979 election – the free play of market forces, an end to the propping up of 'lame duck' industries, the need to restore incentive and enterprise to the economy. It, too, wished to convince the electorate that 'the years of make-believe and false optimism are over. It is time for a new beginning.' Margaret Thatcher had been a member of the Heath Cabinet and had been, without protest, party to all the subsequent U-turns of policy, starting with the decision in February 1971, to nationalise Rolls-Royce rather than let it go bust, and continuing with the highly 'interventionist' 1972 Industry Act and the introduction of a full-blown prices and incomes policy. Mrs Thatcher's supporters were sure that she had a much clearer and more powerful vision of how the new beginning would be achieved than Heath had ever had and that her will and her determination to see it through were equally much stronger. But would they be proved right? And could she communicate that vision to enough others for it to be possible to translate it into a successful political programme? For, just as Mrs Thatcher became leader of the party, not by emerging as a candidate of the party establishment, but by a bold commando raid whilst that establishment was in disarray after the second 1974 election defeat, so she took her party into the 1979 election with a programme that was influenced as much by her personal wishes as by the considered views of the majority of the Shadow Cabinet. Indeed Mrs Thatcher had developed a reputation for 'making policy on the hoof', by speech or television interview, partly because she knew that this was the only way to pull the party's collective leadership in her direction on key issues like the trade unions. What, then, were the essentials of this vision and how had it come to her?

Ironically in the light of subsequent events, it was Heath who, after the first 1974 election defeat, gave Sir Keith Joseph permission to set up with Mrs Thatcher his own research unit, the Centre for Policy Studies, with its own staff and independent finance. Joseph, whom many thought at that time the most likely person to challenge Heath for the leadership, felt that the Conservative Central Office was too imbued with traditional Conservative thinking; and that the other focus of political thinking within the party, the then still independent Conservative Research Department, had an irredeemably left-wing ethos. With Joseph as chairman and Alfred Sherman as director of studies the Centre for Policy Studies became the 'think tank' for the new philosophy.

Alfred Sherman was an inspired choice to run such an institution. As a younger man he had been a socialist. He is no respecter of persons, or institutions. He makes (and is not afraid to make) enemies. He is described by friends as a 'really fizzy man' and he had come to agree with the underlying idea, which Margaret Thatcher had expressed as early as 1968 in a lecture during the party conference, that the power of the state over the individual was growing and should be reduced, that government was becoming remote from people and that this should be tackled not by making it less remote but by reducing the area in which government took decisions for people.

In fleshing out this philosophy for Mrs Thatcher, Sir Keith Joseph played a central role. He is genuinely intellectual in his approach to politics. The early evidence of his own conversion away from the mainstream of post-war British politics was contained in a major speech delivered at Preston on 5 September, 1974.

Joseph had agonised over this speech for weeks, asking for advice on it in draft from a wide array of politicians, economists and journalists. It was said that he had shown it to Heath. If so, it cannot entirely have pleased him. For Joseph, making a major and controversial statement on the economy although he was then the shadow spokesman on home affairs, in effect confessed that post-war economic policy in general and the Heath government's economic policy in particular had been entirely wrong. He accepted his full share of collective responsibility for the past, but for the future it must be made clear that the only imperative was the control of inflation. And this could only be achieved by the strict control of the amount of money in the economy. A future Conservative government must embrace this truth, whatever the cost in the short term to employment, living standards, new investment or political support.

The speech was not entirely clear or consistent, for it bore the mark of many drafting hands and Joseph himself was still in the process of conversion. But it was obviously intended as an attempt to capture the Tory policy stage with a new doctrine. (His chances of becoming in consequence the next leader of the party were virtually destroyed in the following month when he delivered a companion speech on social policy. Its message, the need for a return from the permissive society to one which honoured older values, was ruined by the remark, which many found inexcusably offensive, that the country's stock was being threatened by a higher birth rate among poor families and parents of low intelligence.)

Mrs Thatcher, herself, had never shown signs of being a particularly original thinker. On economic policy, which for the first time since the war was again becoming a major intellectual and political battleground, she had at that stage no views at all. She became Keith Joseph's disciple in these matters and, after he himself stood aside in the leadership contest, he remained the new leader's principal tutor in these matters. He provided for her an intellectual framework that fitted her political instincts perfectly. Those instincts told her that the majority of people in Britain had become disillusioned with the Welfare State and were increasingly hostile to many of the activities of trade unions.

The purpose of the great post-war social and economic experiment that laid the foundations of the Welfare State had been, in the words of the 1942 Beveridge report, a comprehensive policy of social progress through a *collective* attack on the 'five giants' of Want, Disease, Ignorance, Squalor and Idleness. Its weapons for more than thirty years had been the *central* provision of public services, such as the National Health Service; and the ever increasing use of 'transfer payments' to individuals, such as state pensions and child benefits. This was combined with a clear assumption by both political parties, that the government had a duty to become involved in solving social, economic and industrial problems when they arose.

The reaction against more than three decades of welfare policies in this country had displayed many of the characteristics of the *petit bourgeois*, small shopkeeper, anti-taxation Poujadiste protest movement in France in the 1950s. Mrs Thatcher understood the increasingly hostile response to high rates of marginal taxation, rising domestic rates, and the encroachment of a bureaucratic, form-filling state machine on the part of professional managers and executives, small independent shopkeepers, business men, professional people, and, above all, the self-employed. After all, for 20 years she has represented a constituency, Finchley in North London, where over half the adult population falls into these categories, almost four times the national average.

Sensing this growing dissatisfaction with the Welfare State, the Institute of Economic Affairs conducted from 1963 to 1978 a series of investigations into public attitudes in this area. It looked at the vast and ever growing structure that takes in money by taxes and pays out money by providing goods and services and by paying pensions, benefits, subsidies and the rest, and asked whether what it did either reflected or respected the individual preferences of most people. Secondly, it asked whether, even on its own terms, the system was worth 'all the effort, expense, bureaucratic ballast, disincentive to effort, tax avoidance and evasion, tension between tax-payers and tax-gatherers, aggrandisement of government, monopolisation of personal services, suppression of innovation, strengthening of trade union hegemony, debilitation of the family, loss of talent by emigration?'

The words come from a 1979 IEA publication, *Over-ruled on Welfare*, in which Ralph Harris and Athur Seldon brought together the results of these surveys. There is no doubt that ideas generated by them and associated work published by the IEA on policies for housing, health, education, local government and other issues had a profound effect on the thinking of Keith Joseph and Mrs Thatcher. From 1975 onwards the notions contained in IEA pamphlets became an increasing part of their own political philosophy. The technique employed by the IEA surveys was a combination of conventional market research and conventional opinion polling, designed to establish the preference of individuals and families in areas where, because of the non-market nature of the services provided by the Welfare State, these preferences could not be expressed by people 'voting' with their own money.

Their findings gave support to Mrs Thatcher's political instincts and strengthened her view that she was more in touch with the feelings of ordinary people than some of her colleagues. For example, they found that by 1978 almost 60 per cent of those in their sample thought that it would be a good idea to have a referendum to reduce taxation in this country to some maximum proportion or limit. This in itself was not surprising, for no-one likes paying tax. The breakdown within the total was, however, surprising. First, Labour supporters were as much in favour of the proposition as Conservatives. The young were more in favour than the old. Most surprising of all, the lower social and occupational groups (C2,D,E) were significantly more in favour of the idea than the upper groups (AB,C1). The greatest support was found amongst those in occupational class C2, broadly the skilled working class. It seemed that those most opposed to high taxes were not necessarily those with the highest incomes, but those whose incomes had been rising most rapidly in relative terms.

When the surveys asked whether, given the choice, people would like to pay more tax and get better public services, or pay less tax and have to spend more money on certain services themselves, they found large majorities in favour of opting out of parts of the Welfare State. Notably, by 1978, over 80 per cent of the samples were in favour of ending the virtual state monopoly in health and education. Over half thought that they were in favour of a system whereby, for education and health care, the state would provide a voucher that could be cashed in with any school, or doctor or hospital, but which required the individual to pay one third of the full cost. Once again the lower occupational groups were found to be as emphatic as the higher groups in not wishing to pay higher taxes for better services. In the case of health, half of all Labour supporters, as well as two thirds of Conservative supporters, were in favour of such a scheme. Above all, the surveys showed the strength of the trend of opinion in these directions, particularly since about 1970. In 1963 half the sample was prepared to pay higher taxes to get better state education. By 1970 that figure was down to 44 per cent; by 1978 it had plummeted to a mere 15 per cent. In short, the surveys confirmed the view expressed by Raymond Fletcher, the Labour MP from the Derbyshire mining constituency of Ilkeston, who wrote as early as 1966 in *The Times* that '... the workers ... have little enthusiasm for an expansion of the social wage at the expense of their individual wage packets ... In the last two decades their collective aspirations have waned and their individual aspirations have waxed ...' It was this change in attitude that Mrs Thatcher sensed could give her radical brand of Toryism a political attraction that could be the basis of an entirely new departure in post-war British politics.

Mrs Thatcher also sensed to a greater extent than most of her senior colleagues the way in which the British class structure has become less clear-cut in the decades since the war; and sensed the political consequences of these changes. If ever there had been truth in the idea that Britain was divided into three main social classes, upper, middle and lower, by the mid-1970s the reality was much less simple and much less politically predictable. First, traditional unskilled, or semi-skilled, manual work is a much reduced proportion of total employment. Secondly, the patterns of the relationships between social status and income have changed. In the late 1970s skilled workers, for example miners, were in large numbers earning more than, say, £200 a week, or £10,000 a year and more. Self-employment has become increasingly widespread, transferring down the social scale attitudes and political demands previously confined to the self-employed professional classes. Patterns of house ownership, car ownership, savings, holidays have all changed over the decades when related to the job being done by the head of the family. And with these changes there has developed unnoticed by most politicians a changed public attitude towards the traditional purposes and practices of the Welfare State.

Mrs Thatcher seems also to have been more aware of another aspect of the same phenomenon. While the emergence of what has been called an 'industrial bourgeoisie' has spread more widely what have previously been thought of as right-wing attitudes on, say, the subject of taxation, so the same process has caused the professional and middle classes to feel that their financial and social differentials have been eroded from below. In such circumstances the middle classes have behaved as any group does when it feels its differentials being eroded. They have become socially and politically militant against the forces that seem to be responsible for this move towards egalitarianism. This has produced a backlash against many equalising aspects of the traditional political system, from opposition to comprehensive schools, to resentment of high income taxes.

All these factors have combined to produce a philosophy of 'social Darwinism'. This is a view that compassion and egalitarianism have been carried in our society to the point where they are doing serious damage to the whole, that the balance needs to be swung back to a greater acceptance that a healthy society and economy need to be based on the survival and encouragement of the fittest. Feeling herself to be a self-made person from humble origins, daughter of a grocer, scholarship and grammar school girl, made good by determination and industry, Mrs Thatcher was admirably placed both to understand and to give expression to this mood. A party that promised to get the government and its taxes and its restrictions off the back of people who wanted to make their way in life was bound to be attractive to a broad spectrum of people, who might well not have been traditional Tory voters. The result was the paradox that, while Mrs Thatcher's rather abrasive projection of 'right-wing' attitudes and policies, including those on hanging, immigration and Rhodesia, sometimes upset traditional upper and middle class Tories and strengthened the traditional support within professional and academic circles for the Labour party, it was in fact her wing of the Conservative party that had a surer feel for the aspirations and prejudices of ordinary people.

In addition, in Opposition Mrs Thatcher had refused to ignore the open wound within the party inflicted by the battle over the 1971 Industrial Relations Act and defeats inflicted on the Heath government by the miners in 1972 and 1974. The centre and left of the Conservative party had drawn the conclusion that the problems of industrial relations could not be tackled constructively by legislation and that, as a matter of practical politics, a future Conservative government must avoid a confrontation with the trade union movement as a whole, or with individual powerful unions. This view was well expressed by Sir Ian Gilmour in 1974, after the miners had forced Heath into the election which he lost. He wrote, 'The voters do not want perpetual confrontation between government and unions, any more than they want the unions to be the effective government... The future laws relating to industrial relations can be largely omitted from Conservative policy during the election campaign and the early years of the next . . . government. . . The resulting public tranquillity, which is always a Tory aim, may override the disadvantages.'

Mrs Thatcher never liked this policy of appeasement. Her determination to project herself as the leader of the party that would 'do something about the unions' grew steadily, above all as the winter of 1978-9 progressed and the depth of public disquiet at union activities became even more apparent. That winter of Jim Callaghan's discontent fed the public with a daily diet in the newspapers and on television of garbage strikes, hospital strikes, train strikes, power disruption, even local authority crematorium strikes (which allowed emotive phrases about the unions preventing us even from burying our dead). Shop stewards, unofficial organisers, pickets, militant trouble makers and incompetents were all presented in the most unattractive light. It created a situation to which the politician in Mrs Thatcher knew that she must respond. She and the Conservatives were successfully able to portray the Callaghan government as being a lame duck administration in its closing stages, overwhelmed by events and in pawn to the unions. In doing so, however, she aroused considerable public expectation that the incoming government would be looking for a more effective way of curbing union power.

These attitudes towards taxation, public spending, trade unions and strikes, however, were based simply on a politician's gut feeling for political issues. The function of Joseph's Centre for Policy Studies was to place these gut feelings within some kind of coherent intellectual framework. The theoretical framework that came out was a restatement of the ideas of the 18th-century Scottish philosopher, Adam Smith. These centred on the beneficial effects of market forces, as against the stifling effects of state intervention in the economy. Here the message from the Centre for Policy Studies chimed closely with the output of the Institute of Economic Affairs, which for over twenty years under its co-directors, Ralph Harris and Arthur Seldon, had been sponsoring unfashionable polemical pamphlets in favour of policies based on giving people free choice in the market place. The recurrent theme in all of this writing was that millions of individuals taking decisions within a framework of choice for themselves would produce a more efficient, freer and a less unhappy society than one in which, on the basis of policies decided by government, benefits are handed out in kind in a way which precludes choice in the market. Using this resurrection of classical British economic philosophy, the

IEA and others mounted a sustained attack on the ways of the Welfare State. Instead of the existing range of means-tested benefits, the poor should be given money which they should be free to spend as they liked. Instead of free education, parents should be given vouchers, which they could 'spend' at institutions of their choice. (Incidentally, the fact that the independent University College at Buckingham is entirely fee-paying and outside the system of state finance for university and higher education explains the special affection in which it is held by IEA adherents.) Instead of monopoly industries in the public sector, others should be allowed to compete in order to give consumers a genuine choice. Since they are a labour monopoly, the powers of the unions to resist market forces should be curtailed. In short, it was a message that the whole of the post-war social and economic system should be re-examined. It was a message that Keith Joseph and Mrs Thatcher found personally and politically attractive.

But this involved a paradox. For in adopting these ideas, Mrs Thatcher was turning the Conservative party into a radical party, in contrast to Labour, which was manifestly projecting itself as the party of the status quo. As a result the Conservative party went into the election as the party of change, Callaghan as the safe Baldwinesque figure, asking for support on the basis that, with him at the helm, nothing would change, no dangerous experiments would be tried. For the first time in living memory, it was the party of the right and not the party of the left that was proposing major change on the basis of a strong ideology. In the eternal conflict between the concept of liberty and the concept of equality, Mrs Thatcher had clearly committed her party to a major push in the direction of liberty of the individual, a rolling back of the carpet of bi-partisan politics that had developed in the 35 years since the end of the war. By the time the 1979 manifesto was drafted, the focus of this new political approach was centred on a reduction of personal tax, increasing incentives to work, curbing the power of the unions, reducing the size and scope of government to give it a leaner and a sharper edge, and the transfer of as much commercial and industrial activity as possible from the public to the private sector of the economy. In all of this Mrs Thatcher projected herself as being part of a wider international 'swing to the right' and rejection of post-war social democratic ideas. This swing was symbolised by events such as Malcolm Fraser's victory over the Australian Labour party in 1975, the Swedish social democrats under Olof Palme losing power in the same year, after 44 continuous years in office, and the voters in California deciding in a celebrated referendum in June 1978 in favour of Proposition 13 on their ballot papers, which put an absolute limit on the tax levels that the state government could impose, changeable only by two-thirds majority of both houses of the California legislature, thus forcing it instantly to cut its spending programmes.

Mrs Thatcher may have been right about the tide of politics. Certainly, she was right about the tactics of the election. Her problem, however, was that she had not persuaded enough of the party establishment to swim with that tide. That establishment still considered that it was heir to the work done after the 1945 election disaster to create the Conservative party that came back to hold power for thirteen consecutive years up to 1964. In their view, the shock of the 1945 Labour landslide had allowed the younger men in the party, under the leadership of figures like Churchill, Butler, Eden, Macmillan and Woolton, to break the party free from its pre-war image, to bring it to terms with the social and economic changes that had taken place since 1914, to get away from the idea of the Tory party as the party of hard-faced businessmen, away from the bitterness of the 1926 General Strike and mass unemployment and all the social injustices stemming from *laisser-faire* economics and class confrontation. All these ideas were later expressed in a letter to *The Times* in February 1980 from Lord Alport, Deputy Speaker in the House of Lords and a former Conservative minister. He concluded with the following paragraphs, which concisely express the unease in traditional Tory circles about Mrs Thatcher:

> What concerns the Tory Democrat section of the party, who are now denounced as 'wet', is that the 'hard-faced' element, whose attitudes derive from nineteenth century Whig traditions in politics and economics, now appear to be again in control of the country's and the party's destiny.
>
> All parties in a democracy are to some extent coalitions and there is room for a variety of different points of view among their supporters. But a Conservative government in the 1980s which ceases to be 'Tory Democrat' based, which loses the support of the working population and forgets that the only reason why it is now installed in Westminster is because its predecessors after 1945 revolutionized the social and economic attitudes of the

party of the inter-war years, is going to land itself and the country, sooner or later, in big trouble.

Mrs Thatcher was certainly the first person anywhere near the top of the Conservative party to acknowledge the existence of the new 'radical right' and to produce a programme and a political style that appealed to it. She gave symbolic form to this acknowledgment by giving a life peerage in the first Honours List of her administration to Ralph Harris in recognition of the IEA's two decades of steady propaganda in favour of free market economics, in conditions of near exile in a kind of intellectual Siberia. If, however, she was marching in step with a majority of rank and file Conservative voters in the country, when she came to power in May 1979 she had still not convinced the party hierarchy, nor the majority of Tory MPs, nor (most important of all) the majority of her Cabinet. The consequence of this tension is one of the main themes of Mrs Thatcher's first year.

Chapter 2

Humble and obedient servants

> The British civil service . . . is a beautifully designed and effective braking mechanism.
>
> *Shirley Williams, 11 February, 1980, in a lecture to the Royal Institute of Public Administration.*

> . . . the civil service is a bit like a Rolls-Royce – you know it's the best machine in the world, but you're not quite sure what to do with it. I think it's a bit too smooth: it needs *rubbing up* a bit.
>
> *R. A. Butler, quoted in Anthony Sampson's* Anatomy of Britain Today.

PRIME MINISTERS AND POLITICIANS PROPOSE, but when they come to dispose they have to work through the machinery of the permanent Civil Service. This country is unique in the fact that an incoming government is expected to accept as its closest advisers civil servants who were giving politically sensitive advice to its opponents the week before.

It is an extraordinary system and the Civil Service is an extraordinary and a powerful institution. It works on the basis of a constitutional doctrine that does not and cannot correspond to reality. The doctrine is that the country is run by elected politicians and an elected government; that the function of the Civil Service is to provide ministers with information and advice and to present them with a variety of options so that they can come to their policy decisions; and that, once those decisions have been taken, the Civil Service will loyally carry out instructions, even if it disagrees with them. In practice, as every civil servant and every minister knows, and as every incoming government soon discovers, it does not work that way.

In the first place, any institution, above all one made up of such

exceptionally able people as the administrative grade of the Civil
Service, develops a cohesion, continuity, doctrine, loyalty of its own.
In the second, the Civil Service is permanent, while ministers come
and go, rarely doing the same job for more than a couple years before
moving on or out, or back into Opposition. And, in the third, the
volume of business going through the Whitehall machine is so vast and
the number of ministers so few that even an insomniac celibate can
only be aware of the smallest part of it. The art of 'handling my
minister' is, thus, an art of central importance to any senior
bureaucrat.

The arrival of Margaret Thatcher's government in the corridors
of Whitehall in May 1979 was the biggest jolt that the Civil Service had
experienced in living memory. For a while the whole Whitehall system
almost visibly juddered. The only recent experience with which it
could even be compared was the arrival of Harold Wilson's first
government in 1964, when the Civil Service had been required to
unthink the habits to which it had become accustomed in 13
continuous years of living with Conservative ministers.

There had been certain local difficulties and some pyrotechnic
episodes on that occasion. The clash between the mercurial Marcia
Williams, the Prime Minister's 'political and personal secretary', and
the incumbent Principal Private Secretary at No. 10, Derek Mitchell,
resulted in his being banished to the embassy in Washington,
effectively blighted the remainder of his Civil Service career and has
become part of the myth and legend of Whitehall. Normally, however,
senior civil servants have a highly tuned sense of what is and what is not
'politically possible' for an incoming government and an impressive
ability to anticipate 'political requirements', even before they have
been articulated. The letter and the spirit of an incoming party's
manifesto and other pre-election commitments are examined and
normally well digested in advance. The problem on this occasion was
that, as with a majority of Mrs Thatcher's Shadow Cabinet, the
majority of senior civil servants neither understood nor believed in the
dogmas of the Prime Minister and those close about her.

It was a culture shock. The elite administrative grade of the Civil
Service in Whitehall has come to think of itself as the guardian and
trustee of national continuity, a self-appointed role that in other
politically less stable countries is often assumed by the army. It was
now faced with an incoming government that purported to believe in

an entirely new model of how the economy worked and how social policy should be conducted. The Prime Minister and a small group of sympathetic ministers were attempting a revolution, albeit a very peaceful and British one. They were arguing in effect that in the decades since the war the Civil Service had failed in its duties as national trustee, that its ideas and advice had proved bankrupt, that now was the time for an entirely new approach.

As Shirley Williams and others before her have observed, the instincts of senior civil servants are opposed to revolution and sudden change. The dominant educational influence on those from whom they recruit their successors is still Oxbridge and the liberal arts. The values of that system impregnate Whitehall completely. It is a tradition that gives absolute pride of place to analysis and criticism, rather than to creative and original work, that rates the classicist and the art historian above the engineer and the artist, the pure mathematician above the applied mathematician. The grain, indeed, goes even deeper. Senior civil servants, once they have been recruited, for the most part straight out of the universities, spend the rest of their professional lives as part of an inbred society, akin in many ways to a monastic order. It has its own rules, priorities and values, quite different from those of other occupations. Within this order, safety and soundness are the main care of the ambitious man or woman. An entrepreneur can fail in his first project and still become a tycoon. A novelist can write a dozen unpublished works before achieving a literary reputation. But a civil servant who makes one serious mistake is a marked man.

Not surprisingly, therefore, the Civil Service is an inherently conservative institution. What is more, very able men with very clear analytical faculties are understandably prone to think that any new suggestion from outside is unlikely to be of merit, because otherwise they would have thought of it themselves. With Mrs Thatcher's government the critical aversion was all the stronger because the proposed new ideas were clearly being championed by politicians of very little ministerial experience.

Given the likely problems of the relationship between the incoming government and the mandarins of Whitehall, it is surprising that Mrs Thatcher did not decide on some radical experiments in the way in which she proposed to operate the machinery of government. When a Prime Minister enters No. 10, on the day after winning an election, the supportive cocoon of the government machine is rapidly spun about him or her. Unless he or she insists on doing things in a new way from the beginning, the permanent officials are bound to dig deeper into their central and privileged positions.

An incoming Prime Minister in the first moments gets advice from the Secretary to the Cabinet, one of the triumvirate of posts at the top of the Home Civil Service, and from the Principal Private Secretary in the Prime Minister's private office, a post invariably occupied by someone in mid-career, clearly identified as being a Whitehall high flier. On some occasions in the past, for example when Robert Armstrong, the present Secretary to the Cabinet, was doing the job, the Principal Private Secretary could be a source of forceful advice to the Prime Minister, differing from that coming from the Secretary to the Cabinet. (Indeed it is widely said in Whitehall that the outgoing Secretary to the Cabinet, Sir John Hunt, was unhappy about Armstrong's eventual promotion to succeed him in 1979 for this very reason.) When Mrs Thatcher came to No. 10, her private office was run by an able civil servant, Kenneth Stowe, who had come to No. 10 via the Cabinet Office and was, therefore, from Sir John Hunt's 'stable'. The same applied to his successor in June, Clive Whitmore.

Since, on the face of it, it was unlikely that civil servants who had advised, devised and carried out policies for previous Labour and Conservative governments could say a collective *mea culpa* as easily as Sir Keith Joseph in 1974 and set off energetically in an entirely new direction, most Whitehall watchers expected Margaret Thatcher to make sure that there was a substantial injection of new, politically oriented thinking into Whitehall and Cabinet Office structure. From the very start, taking official advice, she did the exact opposite. She accepted a strict construction of the division of role between politicians and officials and she set about playing the game by the letter of the Whitehall rules.

Looking back on her first year in office, this was almost certainly a mistake from her point of view, and one which reduced the impact of the policies she was trying to get across. It made her administration in that first year curiously insensitive to the political context in which it had to operate. It partly explains the difficulty, which by the spring of 1980 she was admitting was damaging politically, of 'getting the message across to the people'. It certainly explains the feeling, abroad in Conservative circles by the late summer of 1979, that the Civil Service was somehow obstructing the government's will.

Mrs Thatcher's first surprising decision was to reduce the size of the non-Civil Service policy unit within No. 10 and substantially to change its role. Under both Wilson and Callaghan this policy unit had been run by Bernard Donoughue, a political scientist from the London School of Economics. He had direct access to the Prime Minister and a staff that fluctuated between five and nine. Its function was to ask politically motivated questions and provide politically sensitive advice to the Prime Minister, in part to supplement and in part to act as a check against the information and advice coming through the normal Civil Service machine. Donoughue's influence and usefulness were increased by his personal links with the political advisers to individual ministers in Whitehall departments. It provided a kind of informal information system, reaching out from Downing Street through the whole of Whitehall. It gave the Prime Minister extra, non-Civil Service eyes and ears.

It was widely expected (not least by himself) that the Donoughue job under a Thatcher government would go to Adam Ridley, a 38-year-old economist, who had worked on the Opposition's economic policy at the then still independent Conservative Research Department. So wide-spread was this assumption that Bernard Donoughue, clearing out his office on the morning after the election, left him a friendly note and a welcoming bottle of whisky.

He got neither the note nor the whisky because the job went instead to John Hoskyns, a 51-year-old ex-soldier, who had built up and then sold a successful computer consultancy company. He had been introduced to Keith Joseph and Margaret Thatcher some three years before through the Centre for Policy Studies and had become an increasingly close adviser to Mrs Thatcher in the run-up to the election, particularly on the broad strategy of how policies should be presented. To the annoyance of some like Jim Prior, Mrs Thatcher had invited Hoskyns to attend meetings of the Shadow Cabinet before the election. During the election itself, he was much involved in the tactical campaign decisions and in writing her speeches. By allowing Ridley to think that he would get the policy unit job, Mrs Thatcher revealed a human though unbusinesslike aversion to making and communicating awkward personal decisions. Indeed, only days before the election, Hoskyns was asked whether he would be prepared to do the job in harness with Ridley. He made it clear that he would not, and so Sir Geoffrey Howe was told that he had to take Ridley with him as a special adviser to the Treasury instead.

The Hoskyns policy unit, however, was to be a different animal from its Labour predecessor. It was physically removed to a more remote part of No. 10 and Donoughue's old office was occupied instead by David Wolfson, the nephew of Sir Isaac Wolfson, founder of Great Universal Stores, who had come to Mrs Thatcher's attention when he was advising the Conservative Central Office on the use of computers, and whom she took to No. 10 as her 'chief of staff'. Wolfson's office became the main conduit by which papers, ideas and requests intended to by-pass the Civil Service machine and the official private secretaries could be got to the Prime Minister. In that sense Wolfson became at once a key figure at Mrs Thatcher's court. But he was not concerned as such with the formulation of policy. Indeed the very fact that within a matter of months a senior official described him as 'pure gold' was evidence that the Civil Service saw him as an ally and not as a threat. No civil servant ever called Marcia Williams 'pure gold' while Harold Wilson was Prime Minister.

Hoskyns began as a one-man operation. In July he was joined by Norman Strauss, on secondment from Lever Brothers. The two hoped their channels of communication to ministers whom they knew personally from the Shadow Cabinet would prove effective when needed. Later still the unit was increased by the addition of a civil servant, Andrew Duguid, who had been in Keith Joseph's private office at the Department of Industry. Even so, it was a remarkably small group for the task that it set itself, namely ensuring that the government as a whole had a clearly defined strategy for changing society and seeing that it stuck to it despite the urgent pressures of daily events.

In fact two or three people are far too few to enable a policy unit to achieve even the minimal monitoring of the work of the myriad of Cabinet committees, ministerial and official, required to ensure that a strategy is being followed. Very soon departmental officials were bold enough to write minutes to the effect that particular policy unit initiatives, such as the need for concerted policies to re-invigorate the 'enterprise economy' were 'getting nowhere fast'. Senior civil servants disliked the criticism of past performance that the whole policy unit approach implied. Relations soon became strained, with permanent officials accusing the policy unit of being responsible for 'leaks', and the unit correctly believing that it was being obstructed by the machine. The policy unit suffered from a further weakness in that it contained no specific expertise about economics. Hoskyns was a successful entrepreneur. Strauss had strong ideas about how to manage the process of change within institutions. In the event the critical decisions of domestic policy that dominated Mrs Thatcher's first year were concerned with the economy. In this area, the policy unit was not in a position to make a confident and effective contribution of its own.

In addition Mrs Thatcher had accepted from the start a decision to reduce the number of special and political advisers available to ministers. The Civil Service has always disliked political advisers since they were first introduced in significant numbers in the 1964 Wilson government. They find it a nuisance that ideas and advice which have not been officially filtered, can get directly to ministers. Even more, they dislike the way in which special advisers enable busy ministers to get information and develop personal positions on politically sensitive issues outside their direct departmental responsibilities, thus often upsetting the delicate balance and operation of the Whitehall machine.

But if ever there was an incoming administration that needed more not less political advisers it was Margaret Thatcher's. Ministers in the key departments would need all the help they could get in persuading their civil servants that there was a viable alternative way of doing things. They would also need help, individually and collectively, to find a way of getting this message across to a wider public. The electorate had certainly voted for change after that fearful winter of 1978–9, but it equally certainly did not understand the nature or the effect of the new nostrums that were being adopted.

Mrs Thatcher, however, was persuaded that her government ought to set an early example in Whitehall manpower saving and so advisers, to the delight of the Civil Service, were reserved for Cabinet members alone. Only after heated argument was a grudging exception made for Nigel Lawson, the Treasury junior minister, who was also allowed one. The total number of full-time special advisers to departmental ministers was reduced to under ten, three of them in the Treasury.

Equally, if ever there was a case for an incoming administration to have as a chief press secretary at No. 10, someone personally close to the Prime Minister and in sympathy with the party line, it was Mrs Thatcher's. Yet once again she took the line of least resistance to the Civil Service. It is true that in the first flush of election victory she appointed a former No. 10 press secretary, Henry James, for six months. When he retired she happily accepted in his place Bernard Ingham, a civil servant from the Department of Energy, previously an information officer there and at the Department of Employment, an ex-journalist who in 1968 had been persuaded to become a civil servant by Barbara Castle when she was Minister of Employment. He had once been a Labour parliamentary candidate and Mrs Thatcher had never met him. There was every reason to suppose that Ingham would make a thoroughly professional No. 10 spokesman, but there were those, in Central Office for example, who thought that a more politically sensitive appointment would have served the cause better.

This willingness on the part of Mrs Thatcher to fall in with the Civil Service's notion of propriety contrasted strangely with the impact of incoming Conservative ministers in particular departments. This impact was not, of course, even. In some departments, like Defence, Agriculture and the Home Office (with its responsibility for law and order), there was no reason for officials to suppose that they would have much trouble with their ministers. At Education, if there was some qualm about the Conservatives' education policy in general, there was the knowledge that this was now shared in large measure by the minister. The problems were clearly centred in those departments where the government's proposed policies seemed to depart most radically from the past bi-partisan consensus that the official Whitehall machine understood and supported. These were the departments dealing with the economy, industry, trade, the trade unions and the Social Security system.

There was, for example, some concern in the upper reaches of the Department of Employment, which, while it does not have quite the same close identity with its clients as, say, the Ministry of Agriculture with the National Farmers' Union, still has to work closely with trade unions. What would happen when officials were switched overnight from working on issues connected with the Employment Protection Act, which extended the rights of workers and unions, to drafting the new government's Employment Bill, which was explicitly aimed at restricting some of those same privileges? In some cases this might have involved personal conflicts of principle, for example in the case of the son of the ex-Labour Chief Whip, Bob Mellish, who was a civil servant in the department. In the event the constitutional doctrine of the civil servant's impartial duty seems to have held, though the fact that Jim Prior, a self-confessed 'dove' in these matters, was the minister may have helped to avoid focusing on the issue very sharply.

The main pressure points were the Department of Industry and the Treasury. The Department of Industry has responsibility for the government's positive policy towards the private sector of the economy and towards most of the nationalised industries. It awaited a government which seemed to take the view that there should be no such active policies and a minister who was the high priest of that doctrine. The atmosphere in the department during May was as a result distinctly edgy. This was not helped by the traditional first meeting between the minister and his senior officials on the day of his appointment. Led by Sir Peter Carey, the Permanent Secretary, they were anxious to let Sir Keith Joseph know about the serious problems that faced him, ranging from British Steel and British Leyland in the public sector, to Dunlop and the future of the nuclear power industry in the private sector. They were somewhat surprised when Joseph made it clear that he did not think that there was much point in their talking further until they understood his approach to these problems, which was that the government should avoid, so far as it could, becoming involved in them.

He told them as a tutor to his students to go away and read, or read again, certain works which would make it clear how he wanted them to approach industrial policy. His reading list included 29 items. Nineteen of them were pamphlets either from his Centre for Policy Studies, or from the Institute of Economic Affairs. These included contributions by Sam Brittan of the *Financial Times* and Peter Jay, formerly economics editor of *The Times*. Eight had either been written or edited by himself, including a paper entitled *Solving the Union Problem is the Key to Britain's Recovery*. There was a short pamphlet by Colin Clark on *The Political Economy of a Christian Society*, and another, attacking the orthodox American economist Professor J.K. Galbraith, by Sir Frank McFadzean, who was shortly to help Rolls-Royce in a blazing dispute with the National

Enterprise Board. To give balance to the more ephemeral titles on his reading list, Joseph included a few classic works: Schumpeter's *Capitalism, Socialism and Democracy*, published in 1944; de Tocqueville's *Democracy in America*, published in 1835; and, of course, the old testament of the new economics, Adam Smith's *Wealth of Nations*, first published in 1776 though available, it was indicated, in a more recent Penguin edition.

It was an unnerving start, but it was not to last long. By the middle of June his senior civil servants were confident that they had got the guru under control. During the Whitehall arguments about the public spending cuts that preceded the June budget, Sir Keith had been brought round to defending almost all the department's spending programmes. Even with industrial subsidies, the argument that they were necessary because they were available in virtually all our competitor countries seemed to prevail. An important test case was whether or not the new government would continue to allow the aid, which the previous government had authorised, for the infant micro-processor industry, through National Enterprise Board support for a new company, Inmos. The departmental submission, supporting continued assistance, to which he put his name, was so poorly argued that it is reputed to have come back from the Prime Minister with the note 'Really Keith!' But support for Inmos continued nevertheless.

Events turned out rather differently at the Treasury. There the assumption by officials was that the incoming Treasury team could not possibly adhere to its doctrinaire, pre-election positions once the facts of life had been explained. The shock of the first six months was the discovery that they did indeed intend to carry through a controlled 'test to destruction' of the British economy, in order to prove that defeatists within the Treasury were wrong and that there was a possible way, within a reasonably short time, out of the vicious cycle in which we seemed to be caught. And, if Sir Douglas Wass, the Permanent Secretary, seemed to some of his colleagues to be glum at the election result, he had good cause to be so, for his job was in the balance. The reason was a lecture he had given well over a year before, in February 1978, to a society at Cambridge.

By itself the lecture was not exactly sensational. It had been on the subject of 'The Changing Problems of Economic Management' and it looked at the way in which, as seen from the Treasury, these problems had become more complex since 1968, when his predecessor Sir William (now Lord) Armstrong gave a lecture which concluded that 'modern economic policy has clearly been a success'. Wass had rehearsed the ways in which the 'almost Victorian optimism among businessmen, bankers, consumers and government officials' about the future of the economy in the 1960s, reflected in the Armstrong lecture, had given way to discord and disagreement about how to resolve our problems. He had then reviewed the pros and cons of various contemporary suggestions about policy. He did so in the measured terms that one would expect from an experienced and wily civil servant, with many qualifications and without coming to any firm conclusions. Few in his audience at the Johnian Society that evening would have thought that they were witnessing a mandarin putting his job on the line.

But that was precisely what he was doing. It is quite unusual for the head of the Treasury to give lectures in public about economic policy and even more unusual for him to seek publicity for such an event. In this case, his lecture was issued as an official Treasury press release. The inference was drawn, correctly, that Wass wished people to read between the lines of what he was saying. The message being transmitted was that the Treasury at official level had severe doubts about whether any of the 'new formulae (that) have been put forward for the resolution of our collective problems' would provide the answer. Effective solutions were much more complicated and elusive than some newcomers to the game might suppose. In particular, it was naïve in the modern, integrated world to suppose that one country could solve its problems by itself. Equally, it was grossly inefficient to engage in frequent changes in public sector spending programmes, which should, therefore, not be used to regulate the economy. Above all, for a government to adopt some 'arbitrary formula' for deciding what its monetary policy should be 'without regard to the effect of other aspects of policy would be to risk imposing serious costs upon the economy'.

The context of Wass's speech makes clear its impact. First, the Governor of the Bank of England had shortly before made a speech in which he had edged further in public than ever before towards accepting a 'monetarist' formula – the belief that price inflation is caused solely by governments allowing the amount of money in the system to increase too fast, and that it can only be reduced by a steady reduction in the rate at which it is increasing. Secondly, Sir Keith Joseph, Mrs Thatcher and Sir Geoffrey Howe (amongst others) had come to accept this theory as self-evident. Indeed, by the time the Conservative policy document, *The Right Approach to the Economy*, was published in October 1977, it was part of official party policy. After the publicity which the lecture received, Sir Geoffrey Howe was widely reported to have been going around town saying that, when they came to office, Sir Douglas Wass would have to go.

In practice, if Howe had wanted to get rid of Wass, he would have had to make a move at once. It would in any case never have been easy. It would have been seen as a major assault on the principle of the independence of the Civil Service and selecting a replacement for such a senior job would take time. Sir Geoffrey Howe is not that kind of decisive man and the opportunity passed.

The Treasury, however, was in for one serious shock. Howe decided that he would have regular morning 'prayer meetings' of the Treasury ministers without officials present. It was a suggestion without precedent at the Treasury and deeply shocking to every civil servant. It meant that a very junior minister, like the Financial Secretary, had for that moment at least more intimate access to the Chancellor than the most senior civil servant. More hurtfully, it implied that there were secret, political things that the Chancellor and his colleagues did not wish to share, even with their closest professional advisers. Something like it had happened before in the Heath government, when Peter Walker had been running the mammoth Department of Trade and Industry. But then his department had been responsible for functions later split into no less than four independent ministries – Trade, Industry, Energy, and Prices and Consumer Affairs. He had no fewer than eight ministers responsible to him and, though his Permanent Secretary, Sir Antony Part, had objected violently enough at the time, at least in that case there had been a genuine need for some *political* co-ordination of a huge and rambling empire.

But the Treasury is different. There are only five ministers, including the Chancellor. It is a small department. The only possible conclusion is that Sir Geoffrey Howe and his colleagues felt themselves to be the prize-crew of a captured and still potentially troublesome ship, needing to have their private tactical discussions in order to ensure that they remained in control. Indeed, in those first weeks there was surprisingly little direct contact between Treasury ministers and their civil servants, the more surprising for the fact that most of the early decisions were about the budget and the need for quick public spending cuts where official advice on what could be done was critical.

In the course of the year, there was more of a growing together between ministers and their civil servants. There is no evidence that Sir Douglas Wass changed his mind on whether the policies will actually work. But he has, with complete loyalty, done his duty. This was symbolically recognised when he was made Grand Commander of the Order of the Bath, the highest class of knighthood, in the 1980 New Year's Honours List.

The Treasury was forced to swallow one more pill. In October it was announced that from the New Year the Chief Economic Adviser to the Treasury and next head of the government economic service would be a youth of 35 and a complete outsider. Someone leaked the news in advance, presumably in an attempt to stop it happening. The choice was Terry Burns, from the London Business School, where working for the principal, Professor Jim Ball, he had established a considerable reputation as a monetary economist, with forecasts published over the years in the *Sunday Times*. The pill was bitter quite as much because an outsider (and one so young at that) was being made the titular head of the entire corps of over 380 professional Civil Service economists as because of his known low opinion of the Treasury forecasting system. Only a minority took the contrary position that, if ministers had an entirely novel view of how the economy should operate and inflation could be conquered, it were better that they should have a chief economic adviser who understood what they were talking about.

As Mrs Thatcher's first year wore on, there were increasingly clear signs of the tension between her government and the centre of the Whitehall Civil Service machine. There were, for example, many more press leaks about what was going on than is usual under a Conservative government. The rate of leaks (or openness of government) has tended to increase in any case since the introduction in Whitehall of direct dial exchanges, which mean that someone outside can ring an official's telephone extension directly, without going through a manual switchboard. But the 1979 leak rate was far higher than that, indicating a situation where officials were in many instances deeply unhappy about what was going on and anxious to stop it.

In the same way, officials often adopted a curiously remote form of words when answering questions. Instead of phrases like 'the policy is . . .' or 'we are doing it because . . .' the enquiring journalist heard phrases like 'ministers believe that . . .' and 'ministers are operating on the basis of a model which leads them to suppose that . . .' It all served to indicate that the mandarin class was in a state of suspended disbelief about the whole nature of the Thatcher Experiment, and wished to distance itself from it, while waiting for the pressures of reality to force the government back to the old choices.

It was bad for morale in the Civil Service that distinguished and senior Permanent Secretaries like Sir Douglas Wass and Sir Peter Carey were clearly being required to 'work their passage' with the new government. There were two further reasons why the Civil Service became uneasy about Mrs Thatcher during 1979. The first was that the populist in her responded to a widespread public dislike of what was seen as the privileged position into which the Civil Service had negotiated itself during the previous six years of almost continuous incomes policy. The second was the apparently arbitrary judgments that she was prone to make about individual civil servants.

In her time at the Department of Education, Mrs Thatcher had established good relations with her bureaucrats. After the Conservatives lost the election, 100 of her senior officials invited her back to the office for a farewell party, a most unusual gesture of respect. Certainly, Mrs Thatcher has never objected to civil servants who stand up to her with argument. On the other hand it was quickly noticed that, as Prime Minister, she had a marked preference for extroverts and an equal tendency to make up her mind about someone on the basis of quite superficial evidence. In particular she seemed ready to write people off as 'wet', even when this conflicted with the Whitehall evidence about their previous careers.

More worrying to the Civil Service from a constitutional point of view was the degree to which she wanted to take a positive role in the promotion of civil servants to senior posts. Appointments at the level of Permanent Secretary and Deputy Secretary in Whitehall are normally made on the recommendation of the Senior Appointment Selection Committee, composed of Permanent Secretaries and chaired by Sir Ian Bancroft, the head of the Civil Service. It it usual for these appointments, except perhaps the few at the very top, to be rubber stamped by the Prime Minister. Margaret Thatcher, by contrast, has taken a keen interest in the process. Several recommendations have been sent back for reconsideration.

Mrs Thatcher has used her own channels to check on individuals. With Treasury appointments in particular, she has asked for notes from the Chancellor on the economic views of candidates. It was even said that, in the case of one Treasury promotion, the fact that the candidate was known to be 'the nearest thing to a monetarist that you will find in the Treasury' was a deciding factor in his favour. Peter Middleton, an exceptionally able 45-year-old, who had been responsible for monetary policy in the Treasury since being private secretary to Anthony Barber and chief press officer to both Barber and Denis Healey, was a somewhat surprising appointment to the job of deputy secretary, dealing with inflation and public finance. He seemed to be getting promotion over the head of other candidates. This and other episodes began to raise the question of whether individual civil servants were in danger of damaging their careers if they expressed views or gave advice that conflicted with the prevailing political doctrine. It is a question that goes to the heart of the constitutional position of an independent civil servant.

At the same time Mrs Thatcher was embarked on a campaign that was of even greater concern to civil servants as a class. A document leaked to the *Sunday Times* in the autumn revealed that one of the priorities established by the Hoskyns policy unit was to 'de-privilege the Civil Service'. It was a task specifically assigned to the Civil Service Department itself.

The main public resentment centred on the fact that, in addition to improving its pay relative to other occupations substantially over the years, the Civil Service had succeeded in 1971 in converting its non-contributory pension scheme onto a basis where the benefits were index-linked to rise with the rate of inflation. In theory the Pay Research Unit responsible for Civil Service salaries is required to deduct an allowance for this considerable attraction, just as it is required to make a discount for the 'job security' enjoyed by civil servants. But in a period of high inflation the promise of a future inflation-proofed pension is literally priceless. No private scheme can make such an offer. Mrs Thatcher's government concluded that the time had come to look again at Civil Service pay and pensions. This was coupled with the feeling that there was no reason why Civil Service manpower should be the only part of the economy where cuts in establishment were not the order of the day. In his second budget speech, the Chancellor made the attack official by announcing that a special independent inquiry would be set up to look into the pensions question.

In short, during Mrs Thatcher's first year, the Civil Service experienced the first systematic assault by any recent government on its inmost citadels. The shock was that the assault had come unexpectedly from a government of the right and not, as long awaited, from the left. It remains to be seen how as a class it will defend its interests.

Chapter 3 | *Double or quits*

In the 1950s, 'Tory freedom' worked . . .
Another 'break for freedom' is needed today . . .

Introduction to The Right Approach to the
Economy, *edited by Angus Maude, October 1977.*

IT OFTEN HAPPENS THAT SOMEONE coming new to a job, instead of
having time to get a feel of it, is faced at once with a critical decision.
So it was with Mrs Thatcher and her Treasury ministers when they
had to decide on their first budget. Simply stated, on the basis of pre-
election promises, the figures did not add up.

Until the summer of 1978, Sir Geoffrey Howe's view had been
that cuts in the standard rate of income tax, however desirable,
would have to wait. The priority was to bring the high upper rates of
tax down to the European average. It had become a central part of
Mrs Thatcher's philosophy that high marginal taxes were not only
wrong morally, but were also a major depressant to better economic
performance. So Sir Geoffrey Howe was preparing his mind for a
budget speech which would say that, however strong his longer term
views on the need to lower the standard rate, he had no option but to
concentrate the limited money immediately available where it would
do most good, namely in cutting the highest tax rates.

By the late summer of 1978 Mrs Thatcher had persuaded him
otherwise. She knew that skilled Midlands industrial workers and
other potential first-time Tory voters would not be impressed by
what a Tory chancellor did for people on 83 per cent marginal tax
rates. So, well before the election, Sir Geoffrey found himself
committed to cuts in the standard rate. Jim Callaghan had
unhelpfully said that, if returned, Labour would take 3p off the
standard rate; a Tory chancellor could scarcely do less. Just taking 3p
off the standard rate, however, would lose him £1,500 million of
revenue a year.

On the other side there would, of course, be immediate cuts in
government spending. An election theme had been that small cuts

over a large field all add up, and that much could be saved by cutting out public sector waste and extravagance and by phasing out subsidies to industry. But the existing financial year would already be more than two months old by budget day, 12 June. The scope for cuts that would produce real savings in 1979–80 was obviously limited.

In addition, the party had accepted the theory that, in the words of the manifesto, 'to master inflation, proper monetary discipline is essential, with publicly stated targets for the rate of growth of the money supply.' In the process of equipping herself for No. 10, Margaret Thatcher had met and absorbed the ideas of two distinguished economists, Friedrich Hayek and Milton Friedman. Three years before, she had impressed Hayek with her clear and intellectual interest – for a politician – in the issues of economics. She had dined with Friedman at short notice in 1977. He too noted her detailed interest in his views on money supply and exchange rate policy. By the time she became Prime Minister, though without any original feel for economics, she had decided to accept the broad structure of Friedman's views.

In summary, these are that a rapid increase in the amount of money leads not to a higher level of business activity, except in the very short term, but simply to a higher level of inflation. In reverse, the only way to slow inflation, in his view, is to reduce the rate at which the amount of money is growing. The academic work of Professor Friedman, a Nobel prize winner for economics in 1976, is careful and his conclusions qualified. But he enjoys simplifying his message for politicians, television programmes or the popular prints. For Keith Joseph and Margaret Thatcher it was bewitchingly simple. In countries like the United States and the United Kingdom, Friedman said, the first *transitory* effect on the real economy of an increase or reduction in the rate at which the amount of money in the economy is growing has made itself felt in about six months. The *permanent* effect, which is solely on the level of prices, takes about a further eighteen months to become apparent. The Prime Minister and the Chancellor understood the theory in terms of a game of Monopoly. If you took all the money from a spare set and gave that to the players as well, there would be no basic change in the game, but very soon the prices of Fenchurch Street Station and all the other properties would double.

Having accepted this picture of how an economy operates, the Chancellor was clearly in difficulty. His combined existing commitments would push up the amount that the government needed to borrow in the current financial year. But, in order not to undermine the battle against inflation, that figure ought to come down, not go up. To some extent this had been foreseen. The manifesto had recognised that, even with rising North Sea oil revenues and spending cuts, there would be problems in financing the income tax reductions that were wanted. It declared that 'we must, therefore, be prepared to switch to some extent from taxes on earnings to taxes on spending.' This implied an increase in the rate of Value Added Tax, though as the manifesto was quick to point out not on necessities like food, fuel, housing and transport, which carry no VAT.

There was, however, a technical difficulty. It was logical in terms of the government's philosophy to cut income tax and put up VAT. It fitted the idea that people should keep more of what they earn and then decide for themselves how it should be spent. But increases in indirect taxes could only be imposed after the budget, in the case of VAT from the beginning of July. Cuts in income tax, on the other hand, would all be back-dated to the beginning of the financial year in April.

If Howe set his VAT increases to balance his income tax cuts in a full year, because of missing the first three months with VAT, the net effect in his first financial year would be to increase his deficit by well over £1,000 million. Treasury officials hoped privately that the government would proceed with caution. Mrs Thatcher, after all, had only said during her campaign that the 'first instalments' of the promised income tax cuts would come in the first budget.

This official inclination was strengthened by the forecasts for the economy, prepared before the election. These predicted no expansion at all in the new government's first year. Spending by consumers was even expected to fall. A substantial cut in income tax more than matched in the first year by increased VAT would make things worse, because people would save a proportion of the extra money they got after tax.

Howe's inclination was otherwise. After everything that they had said about excessive borrowing by the previous government, he felt that it would be seen as doctrinal backsliding if the first Tory budget further increased the borrowing figure. This view was strongly shared by Nigel Lawson, who for a junior minister rapidly developed a surprising degree of influence over policy and at least a 'warm line' to the Prime Minister. For her part, Mrs Thatcher wanted the cutting of government spending to start in earnest at once.

For some time the Chancellor did not appreciate Mrs Thatcher's expectations on this score. In fact he and John Biffen, who as Chief Secretary to the Treasury was directly in charge of public spending, were quite pleased when, by the end of the month, they had produced a £500 million package of spending cuts. It was a shock and a lesson to him, when he went with Biffen to report on progress to the Prime Minister. She ticked him off roundly and sent him away saying, 'Come, come Geoffrey. The financial year has only just started. You can do better than £500 million.' This episode taught the Chancellor that in future he must always clear his lines with the Prime Minister in advance. For officials in the Treasury it was even more of a shock. Here, for the first time, was a Prime Minister saying that the largest policy option offered was not big enough and that they must find more. Normal roles had been reversed.

So Howe, Biffen and their officials tried harder and by 12 June had a package that was presented as being worth £3,500 million. The increase consisted largely of an extra £1,000 million to come from the sale of public assets and the hope that still tighter control of existing expenditure programmes would produce a further £1,000 million of savings.

Even so, the circle could only be squared if the government was prepared to abandon caution and raise VAT by previously unthinkable amounts at once. Mrs Thatcher accepted the logic and agreed that VAT, previously charged at 8 and $12\frac{1}{2}$ per cent, should be raised to a new single rate of 15 per cent. On the government's own figuring this alone put $3\frac{1}{2}$ per cent on to the cost of living 'at a stroke'.

Even this was not quite enough. Unlike previous Prime Ministers, from the start Mrs Thatcher called in the Governor of the Bank of England for advice. In part this was probably because she rightly sensed that Gordon Richardson and his officials were more in sympathy with her monetary ideas than the majority at the Treasury.

The Governor's view was that the budget as a whole would not convince the City that the growth rate for money would be kept within a new lower target range of 7–11 per cent over the year ahead. So, to indicate conclusively to the City the government's determination in the matter, Mrs Thatcher reluctantly agreed as well to a 2 per cent jump in the Bank's minimum lending rate (formerly known as Bank Rate) to what would previously have been thought a crisis level of 14 per cent. As it was the Governor's stern advice, the increase was announced by the Bank of England and not as part of the Chancellor's budget speech.

Looking back on that budget as the year progressed, it seemed increasingly to have been a serious mistake. The fact that Mrs Thatcher should have endorsed such a reckless throw is all the more curious because in almost every other area, whatever the personal convictions or prejudices that she brought to No. 10, she began cautiously. Part of the explanation is probably that, in comparison with other areas of domestic policy, Mrs Thatcher had very little understanding of economics. She had diligently taken in lessons at the knees of Keith Joseph, Hayek and Friedman, but she had not acquired the critical capacity to apply tests of common sense when it came to putting ideas into action.

She believed that if controls were removed, incentives restored and top income tax rates cut to 60 per cent, somehow there would be such a home-coming of talent and a liberation of energy in the professional, entrepreneurial and managerial classes that the whole performance of the economy would be uplifted at once. She was to say later, in March 1979 when things had gone sour, that she had never promised the people 'instant sunshine'. That may have been literally true, but there was no doubt that Howe's first budget successfully conveyed the intended message that spring at least had come. Could summer be far behind? The 'break for freedom' in the budget was reinforced by the rapid abolition of pay controls, price controls, dividend controls and, by the autumn, all foreign exchange controls.

The view of most Treasury officials was that, however strong the moral, political or administrative arguments in favour of these policies (and whatever the long term benefits might be) any idea that they would sharply improve the performance of the economy in the short term flew in the face of reason. At best, such a notion could only be based on faith. And faith could not be fed directly into the computer model with which forecasts were produced. The more cynical were saying that the main reason for cutting the top tax rates to the European average was that this would, at least, put an end to the argument about the effect of high tax rates. Mrs Thatcher's view, however, was more positive. She had picked up, via the Institute of Economic Affairs, an idea of an American economist, Professor Arthur Laffer, that lower tax *rates* could actually raise tax *revenues*. She had said as much on television during the election campaign. 'People assume that if you cut rates, you've got to recoup it elsewhere. But this is not necessarily true, as a cut in taxes will lead to *larger* incentives and therefore *larger* output and a *larger* tax take.' This theory was not an operational assumption within the Treasury.

The Prime Minister's relationship to economic policy was different from her relationship to other areas of policy in another important way. In foreign affairs, on trade union law, or energy policy, for example, she was faced with ministers who had, or soon developed, strong views of their own, for which they were prepared to fight. With the Chancellor this was not the case. He too was a lawyer, with a clear ability to master a brief, but on coming to the Treasury no instinctive feel for economics. There were ministers under him, like Biffen and Lawson, who held firm views on the subject. But the Chancellor himself gave most people the impression of behaving towards the Prime Minister as a good country solicitor behaves towards an important client. Provided the client knows what he or she wants and gives clear instructions, these will be more than competently executed. In the absence of such instructions, however, unilateral initiatives of an imaginative kind should not be expected. Within the Treasury he showed soon enough that he was confident in his own judgments, though his officials rapidly sensed that he disliked risking rebukes from the Prime Minister. The only disconcerting thing to them was the way in which he could abruptly switch from his normal, down-to-earth, competent permanent secretary approach to a problem into an almost Messianic echo of the Prime Minister's own doctrines about the way in which Tory freedoms would liberate and transform the economy. The combination of these factors meant that the budget strategy announced by the Chancellor on 12 June was decidedly 'high risk'.

When he rose to present his second budget on 26 March, 1980,

Geoffrey Howe must have been regretting that he had not heeded the voices which ten months before had diffidently suggested that the better course in the long run might be to do things by stages. In retrospect, in deciding on his first big budget package he had failed to take account of two factors, one domestic, one external.

All Chancellors make mistakes. Just as Napoleon forgot Blücher, Howe forgot Clegg. Confronted by a problem to which there is no easy political solution, governments have a tendency to refer it to a new committee. With rising pay demands in the public sector and with his incomes policy in tatters, Jim Callaghan had set up a new six-member standing commission under the chairmanship of Professor Hugh Clegg. It came into being on 7 March, just three weeks before the Callaghan government was brought down. It was a body to which, provided the relevant trade unions agreed, the government could refer public sector pay claims for analysis and recommendation. The commission was called upon immediately to consider the case of manual workers employed by local authorities and universities, ancillary staff in the National Health Service, and ambulance men. Between 7 March and the election on 3 May, the outgoing government made five further references to Clegg. The most significant was the claim by nurses and midwives. Others included claims by university technicians, those working in the supplementary medical professions, municipal airport manual workers and ambulance officers. The recommendations on the first of these pay references were not published until August. During the election campaign Mrs Thatcher had committed herself to accepting whatever Clegg in his wisdom awarded by way of pay increases. When they came to power the Tories continued to refer pay claims to the Clegg commission rather than become directly involved in difficult public sector pay negotiations, even though the Cabinet's public sector pay subcommittee was chaired by Sir Keith Joseph. Teachers' pay, for example, was given to Clegg in July. By the time of his second budget in March, Geoffrey Howe was accusing the Opposition of having left post-dated cheques behind, and claiming that the operations of the Clegg commission would add £2,000 million to the public sector wage bill in the coming financial year.

The overlooked external factor was inflation in the rest of the world. During the winter and spring before the election, the Chancellor and his economic advisers had been so preoccupied with domestic troubles that they came to office with their attention still focused entirely inwards. If they had stopped for a moment to look outwards, they would probably have seen that 1979 was going to be a year of growing inflationary pressures in the whole of the industrial world, not least because even in May it was clear that there would shortly be another substantial increase in oil prices by OPEC countries. In that case the Chancellor might have been more cautious about his VAT increases. Instead of dampening inflationary expectations in the economy, this one element in his first budget gratuitously increased them at a dangerous moment.

These wisdoms of hindsight were still many months off, however, when the government launched into its second major economic task, the preparation of its public spending plans for 1980 and beyond. The manifesto commitment was clear. 'Any future government which sets out honestly to reduce inflation and taxation will have to make substantial economies, and there should be no doubt about our intention to do so.' This time the Chancellor agreed the target with the Prime Minister in advance. They wanted £8,000 million off the existing expenditure plans for the following financial year, 1980–81.

It rapidly became clear that the exercise was not going to be easy. They soon gave up any hope of agreeing at that stage cuts for more than the year ahead. In the first place, ministers in spending departments were pulled two ways. Not without reason, the traditional test of baronial virility for a Cabinet minister is his ability to defend and if possible increase spending programmes for which he is responsible. Now, however, the order of the day was reversed. The Prime Minister was making it clear that credit in her eyes would be won by ministers whose empires contracted. The result for most was a condition close to schizophrenia. For some ministers, though, the problem was easier than for others. Public expenditure cutting is done under an arcane accounting system, which, being only indirectly related to the real world, positively encourages confusion. A 'cut' counts as a cut if there is a reduction in the amount that was allocated to be spent on any programme in the previous year's public expenditure White Paper, in this case the previous Labour government's. Even then, since planning is done in constant prices and not in terms of current money, such a 'cut' is unlikely to mean that in the end less actual money will be spent on the programme.

Thus Michael Heseltine at the Department of the Environment was able to count for virtue substantial cuts which flowed directly from the fact that he had no intention anyway of carrying on with the housing and building land policies, budgeted for by the previous Labour government. These were truly cuts without tears for Heseltine, who could thus give ambiguous replies to questions about whether or not his department had taken more than its fair share of the total.

Biffen's task as Chief Secretary was made more difficult by the fact that Mrs Thatcher clearly disliked having arguments in Cabinet which entailed her having to rule between one minister and another. Under the previous Labour government, the bitter public spending debates came eventually to the full Cabinet, where a spirit of collective responsibility could force each major spending minister to compromise and accept his share of the common burden of misery.

Since Mrs Thatcher refused to allow such matters onto the Cabinet agenda (indeed she allowed no general discussion of economic policy at all in Cabinet during 1979) the Treasury had to simulate a Cabinet framework for its negotiations with individual ministers, deftly or doggedly defending their patches. The chosen device was an ad hoc committee of four Cabinet ministers, the Chancellor, Biffen, John Nott and Lord Soames (the last two being chosen because, at the Department of Trade and the Civil Service Department, they were Cabinet ministers without big spending programmes of their own). One by one during July, ministers in the spending departments brought their proposed cuts for decidedly informal oral examination by this little group in the Cabinet Office. Lord Soames, for example, was heard to remark that for the life of him he could not see why the children of well-off parents should get student grants at all, since he had paid for all his children through school *and* university. And so it went on, department by department.

It soon became clear that the original target of £8,000 million in cuts for 1980–81 was not going to be met. There were a number of reasons. The first was that the area in which the Treasury was allowed to look for cuts had been deliberately and substantially circumscribed. For example, the Chancellor had said in his budget speech that all pensions and Social Security benefits would be increased in November by the full percentage by which prices had by then risen, including allowance for the effect of his budget measures. In future they would be increased at least by the rate of inflation, or more if the economy could stand it. Under pressure during the election campaign, Mrs Thatcher had underlined the manifesto commitment that there would be no reduction in the total scale of resources devoted to the Health Service. Even in education, standards were to be improved, the schools inspectorate strengthened and no savings allowed at the expense of 'teaching in the classroom'. Further, the defence budget was actually to be increased as 'the first charge on the budget of any government over which I will preside'. And more money was to go to those programmes concerned with law and order, the police and the prison services. If all these programmes were to be protected, or even increased, the axe would have to fall very hard on the necks of cows that were not sacred.

The second difficulty was that public spending programmes had been through the wringer several times already in the recent past, particularly in 1976. Apart, therefore, from the easy cuts that came from changed policies, the scope for major savings by cutting out waste and extravagance in the public sector was much more limited than the Prime Minister or Nigel Lawson liked to think. The notion that, if only the careful habits of the corner grocer could be applied to the whole of central and local government, huge sums of money could be saved without cutting the quality of the service provided, is an illusion dear to the heart of every small-town Tory. In this spirit, within a week of the election Mrs Thatcher appointed Sir Derek Rayner, joint managing director of Marks and Spencer, as her adviser on the elimination of government waste.

Rayner had served in government before and was once described as Whitehall's favourite businessman. He made a considerable impact on Whitehall at once. But, even with his experience, with a staff of 30 bright young civil servants and with the full backing of the Prime Minister, Rayner only identified potential economies worth £80 million in a full year, together with one-off savings of a further £55 million from scrapping unnecessary capital projects. These sums are, of course, substantial in their own right, but nowhere near the level necessary to change the basic economic and political problems of finding expenditure cuts of £8,000 million in one year.

The most significant limitation on the July cuts, however, was the Prime Minister herself. She knew what she wanted overall: an

£8,000 million reduction. The politician in her, however, jibbed again and again at actual proposals necessary to achieve that overall target.

Some of the areas where this low threshold of political pain operated were so obvious that no one bothered even to test them. For example, while it was a clear plank of the election platform that the previous government's National Enterprise Board should be cut down to size, there was never any question of touching the Scottish Development Agency, or the Welsh Development Agency, which performed the same functions in Scotland and Wales. The reason for this total illogicality was straight political fear of playing into the hands of the Labour party and the nationalist movements in those two countries.

The same taboo, of course, applied to farmers. There was no sign that even an intellectually rigorous Treasury minister like John Biffen was inclined to take on the battle required to extend the new economic philosophy to agriculture. 'Free market' politicians and economists within the Conservative party have, it seems, never felt compelled to apply to farming the belief that subsidies corrupt and efficiency requires the discipline of the market place.

A Conservative MP, Matthew Parris, who had worked in Margaret Thatcher's private office in the period up to the election, was bold enough in the course of the year to produce a sharp parody of current agricultural policies in a letter to *The Times* that ran:

> Sir, Is it only to me that the solution to British Leyland's problems has occurred?
>
> The Government should lay down a minimum selling price for Leyland motor cars, pitched to ensure a profitable return on the capital invested in the industry. Should the company prove unable to dispose of all their motor cars at this price, the European Commission should intervene to purchase the unsold stock.
>
> These unsold vehicles would be stored at Canvey Island or offered to our enemies at half price.
>
> I hope nobody thinks this is a ludicrous way of dealing with the marketing of a commodity.

The implied criticism of the contradiction between the government's policy toward industry and existing EEC support for agriculture is difficult to answer. But, without being unduly cynical, a Cabinet that contained such substantial farmers as Lord Carrington, Sir Ian Gilmour, John Nott, Jim Prior, Francis Pym, Willie Whitelaw and Peter Walker, whatever its other radical notions, was not a Cabinet likely to overturn more than 40 years of agricultural protection. By the end of her first year, Margaret Thatcher's government and her agriculture minister, Peter Walker, were as it happens, embattled with the National Farmers' Union, but that was a consequence of a wider struggle with the Common Market.

What was surprising was the Prime Minister's extreme sensitivity in particular areas, even within the normal range of political tolerance. Take education, for example, where she knew the details from her previous ministerial incarnation. When the July cutting exercise started, the education budget was asked to make the biggest single contribution: a target cut of 10 per cent, or £1,000 million in round figures. The early shopping list of measures that could achieve this target included two items. The first was an increase in the parental contribution to student grants. The second was a proposal that there should be charges for nursery school places. Both of these proposals fitted perfectly well into the government's declared philosophy. The first, however, was ruled out because it would 'hit people like us, whom we're supposed to be helping'. The second was unacceptable because, as education minister, Mrs Thatcher had presided over a substantial expansion of free nursery provision, especially in deprived urban areas, and refused to have her past success singled out now for charges.

In the end Carlisle saved the education budget from the full force of the cuts. His Minister of State, Lady Young, was his secret weapon. She was close to Lord Thorneycroft, having previously been the power behind the women's section in the Conservative Central Office. At the end of one Thursday Cabinet meeting in July, when it came to lunch time, the Prime Minister announced that they would meet again the following Monday. On Friday, Carlisle and Lady Young went to see the Prime Minister. By Monday the education budget cuts were down from 10 per cent to $4\frac{1}{2}$ per cent.

By late July, agreement had been reached by the Cabinet as a whole. The package was substantially smaller than Mrs Thatcher had wanted at the outset, amounting only to some £3,500 million for

1980–81. The Chancellor wanted to announce the results in a White Paper then and there. This was vetoed by the Prime Minister. If they published a White Paper at once, there would have to be a full debate in the House and the summer recess, already fixed for July 27, would have to be postponed. It would look like a crisis. So she took the decision that they would sit on their cuts and announce them in a normal autumn White Paper, normal, that is, except for the fact that it would still not contain spending plans for the years beyond 1980–81.

This slightly curious procedure may in itself have had an influence on events in the rest of Margaret Thatcher's first year. Since no cuts had been announced, none of the predictable campaigns of protest could really get off the ground on the basis only of more or less reliable leaks in the press. The Civil Service was in fact astonished that there was so little fuss and backlash against what was being proposed. There were rumblings about things like overseas student grants and the external services of the BBC, muted even so because the continued absence of the letters columns of *The Times* made it difficult for the establishment to communicate with itself. But nothing serious. It still remained possible that when local authority rates rose sharply in the spring of 1980, or public baths and libraries began to close early because of lack of staff, the mood would switch. But it had not done so by December. Instead large sections of the Conservative party were in favour of deeper cutting still.

To the civil servants, however, it began to be clear by the autumn that the birds released in June were coming home to roost earlier than anyone had expected. Pay and prices, far from showing lower rates of growth, were clearly accelerating. All the basic economic forecasts were predicting a catastrophic medium term outlook. By the autumn the Treasury's initial forecast was that inflation would have risen to over 17 per cent a year by the end of 1980. This was combined with a picture that indicated output actually dropping by more than 3 per cent in 1980 and further in 1981; unemployment up to 2 million by 1981 and still rising; sharp drops in the profitability of the private sector and so on. Ministers, particularly Nigel Lawson, refused to accept the results of these forecasts, preferring to back their own hunches and ridiculing the past Treasury record in this area. It was impossible for them to accept that this would indeed be an accurate picture of the results of their policies. Officials asked in reply which of the assumptions which led to these pessimistic conclusions ministers thought should be modified. Even when these adjustments were made, the recalculated forecasts were still unpublishable without some 'massaging'.

On top of this, the government, which had hoped by means of a bold June budget, a 2 per cent rise in the minimum lending rate and two attempts to cut public spending, to get up-wind of its problems, now found that it had been swept down again by the tide. Public spending, far from being under control, was higher than ever. This was partly the effect of the Clegg awards, partly because the last Labour White Paper, on which they were basing their calculations, had contained some unrealistically low assumptions, partly because the rise in interest rates themselves had substantially increased the cost of servicing the government's own debt and lastly because their own claims in June had been excessively optimistic. Even their key monetary target for the growth in the money supply was not being met.

Here Mrs Thatcher had herself done serious damage to the credibility of the government's commitment to financial rectitude. It was widely known that she had fought long and hard to stop building societies raising their mortgage rates above $9\frac{1}{2}$ per cent in the summer. Once again she was giving way to the politician in her, knowing the effect of higher mortgage payments on many who had voted Tory, especially on those who wished to become first-time home buyers and on young married couples. In addition, she had a personal involvement, because she had worked out a housing policy for Edward Heath between the 1974 elections, which featured a Tory pledge to bring the mortgage interest rate down to a maximum of $9\frac{1}{2}$ per cent. It was, therefore, only with substantial difficulty that Howe weened her off the idea of paying a Treasury subsidy, or finding some other way of financing the building societies, in return for their not moving their rates up in line with the rest of the money market. Under pressure, the building societies promised to hold the line until January. The episode threw real doubt on her commitment to the Friedmanite principle that control of the money supply was the single essential and that, while the inflationary crisis worked itself out, interest rates must be allowed to find their own level.

The outflow of capital following the abolition of exchange controls in October also made it more difficult for the government to find buyers for its own new gilt edge stock, thus allowing the domestic money supply to expand far faster than the official target range. Professor Hayek, who saw the Prime Minister briefly at about this time, was distressed at the way in which she seemed preoccupied with the politically uncomfortable symptoms of the situation. According to his doctrine, any policy to deal with inflation must put the economy through a 'stabilisation crisis'. Yet here was the Prime Minister disturbed at rates of interest that were still below the going rate of inflation. In his view, the less firm the policy, the longer the crisis would last.

Events finally came to a head in the second week of November. With the failure to sell any government stock at prevailing rates of interest, the money supply could not be contained. The government had only two choices. Either it accepted that, for the time being, there would have to be some relaxation of its targets, or it would have to embark on a crisis package to get the situation under control again.

The Prime Minister and her Chancellor of the Exchequer had thought that they were playing the game for high stakes in June and July when they raised the bank rate to 14 per cent and hoped that they had cut £3,500 million of spending. Now, they had no option but to double those stakes, or admit that their policies had been wrong and quit. On 17 November, the Chancellor acted. Where the markets had expected the Bank of England's minimum lending rate to be pushed up to 15½ or even 16 per cent, Howe tried once again to get properly on top. He put the rate to a quite unprecedented 17 per cent. Meanwhile the government set itself the task of producing a full public spending White Paper by March, which was to take £2,000 million off spending plans for future years. But it went further. In addition, another £1,000 million, was to come off the very next year, 1980–81, which had already been so heavily cut the previous July. This was to be exclusive of anything achieved by way of reducing our net contribution to the EEC. Only this time the Cabinet knew that it could not be done without accepting the necessity of cuts which they had all rejected as politically unacceptable the first time round. This time the knife would cut to the bone.

The first thing that became obvious was that no more substantial savings could be made in programmes where the government itself spent directly on buying goods and services and employing people. This was not a surprising conclusion for the Cabinet to be forced to, since in these areas, with the exception of defence, Britain already spends less per head than most other western industrial countries. If the government was going to find further savings on the required scale, these would have to be in the area of what are known as 'transfer payments', programmes under which the government transfers from the Exchequer monies to other bodies, or to individuals, which they then spend themselves. The pressure to attack this area was the greater because in its previous two attempts to cut spending the government had counted for credit the money raised from the sale of assets. In the short term, living off capital in this way may help to balance the books, but it does nothing to change the underlying current account deficit. Therefore, unless selling off capital assets is seen as a continuous source of income to the government, if it wants to reduce its deficit it must tackle the issue directly.

The two largest blocs in this category of transfer spending are Social Security payments and the central government's rate support grant to local authorities, which by now accounts for some two-thirds of all the money nominally spent by locally elected councils. It was to these two areas that ministers were now forced to turn their attention. The battle started in November and went on until the end of January. As we shall see in Chapter 6, the process was to put the greatest possible strain on the cohesion of Mrs Thatcher's Cabinet and to pose the first real test of her position as Prime Minister. In the end, the government was not able to produce the drastic reduction in the whole profile of government spending on which so much of their hopes for future tax reductions depend.

Once again obvious political inhibitions affected how radical the Cabinet was prepared to be. Michael Heseltine would have been in favour of meeting his target cuts by imposing an overall reduction in the numbers employed by local authorities in all their activities. But, without much difficulty, Carlisle got agreement that there would be no further short-term cuts in education, the biggest single local authority service. Some ministers, too, were sensitive to the charge that the 1979 budget had been a 'class budget' and were, therefore, anxious not to allow the second budget to appear to be a further attack on those in society least able to help themselves. Further, there was a clear election commitment that the value of state pensions would be kept abreast of the rate of inflation.

In the event the government decided to increase the state retirement pension and basic supplementary benefit levels by the amount that prices were expected to rise in 1980. Beyond this, the Cabinet decided to break ground that had previously been considered to be unavailable. They decided that from 1982 sickness payments and unemployment benefits should be subject to income tax. The level of short-term unemployment benefits in future was to be on a flat-rate basis for all eligible, and not related to the unemployed person's previous earnings. Most important of all, it was decided that the level of child benefit could not be increased by the full amount of past inflation. This was a particularly difficult decision, because the child benefit scheme and the assumption that payments under it would keep pace with the rise in the cost of living had become an important part of Tory philosophy. Patrick Jenkin had often spoken in favour of the principle. Since it is a benefit that goes to all families with children, regardless of whether the main wage earner is employed or not, it was seen as a major weapon in the attack on the 'poverty trap', where the Social Security system in combination with the tax system can make a family worse off, even when an unemployed man takes a reasonably well paid job.

These measures were part of a total package that enabled the Chancellor in his March budget speech to indicate that public spending in real terms would fall each year between 1980 and 1984. As previous governments have found, it is one thing to make such statements of policy. It is another to carry them out. The fact that the projections showed substantially greater falls in spending in later years than in the immediate future seemed to be repeating the well-observed phenomenon that cuts tomorrow are always easier to make than cuts today. Combined with the fact that the better part of £1,000 million was counted towards immediate cuts simply on the basis that programmes would be more tightly administered, rather than on the basis of ending specific categories of spending, the figures indicated that the government was still concealing from itself the full difficulty of achieving its chosen goals.

By the time of the second Howe budget in March, the Treasury and most outside forecasters were predicting a severe recession into 1982 and beyond. Conventional economics would have advised the Chancellor to do something to increase the level of demand in the economy. He chose instead to do the opposite. His tax proposals in total promised to take even more money out of the economy, on top of the public spending cuts. The government's whole future was made to rest on the hope that a categorical commitment to reduce the rate of growth of money to 6 per cent a year by 1984, combined with the pressures of the recession itself, would get inflation out of the economy in time for there to be some real economic expansion before the next election. Far from deserting the new economics at the end of her first year, Mrs Thatcher clearly decided to stay in the game and to double the stakes. Since no other set of policies seemed capable of providing an answer, the British economy was to be used in a controlled experiment to see whether Professor Friedman's particular economic theories were right.

Chapter 4 | *The overmighty barons*

> . . . by heaping privilege without responsibility on the trade unions, Labour have given a minority of extremists the power to abuse individual liberties and to thwart Britain's chances of success.
>
> *Conservative 1979 election manifesto.*

> If I am overridden . . . I shall resign. It has not happened to me yet.
>
> *James Prior, Secretary of State for Employment, House of Commons, 5 March, 1980.*

WHEN MRS THATCHER BECAME Prime Minister most of her advisers thought that the first real show-down with the unions would not come until the winter of 1980–81, her second winter. In the event, without proper anticipation, the government found itself having to cope with the consequence of the steel strike within its first eight months. The result was that, in the aftermath of the poor Conservative showing at the Southend by-election in March, George Gardiner, the MP for Reigate, properly expressed the views of a large number of those who had voted Margaret Thatcher into office when he said that the government was paying the heavy price of its timidity in curbing trade union power.

Mrs Thatcher was in large measure personally responsible for the high expectations that her government would at once push the pendulum of trade union law back at least to where it had been before the 1974 Labour government. Some hoped that she would go further. In the period between her becoming leader of the Conservative party and the general election she had conducted a kind of antiphonal dialogue in public with Jim Prior, the shadow employment minister, with her putting forward radical proposals and with him watering them down. Her speeches steadily became more extreme in response to the strikes and scenes of the winter of 1978–9.

In the battle for the election manifesto, Prior won. Although the general tone was that the trade unions were overmighty barons, needing to be brought back under the rule of law, the specific proposals put forward were minimalist: a review of existing legal immunities for trade unions in order to decide how to limit 'secondary' picketing, blacking and blockading; rights of appeal and compensation for those losing their jobs because of the operation of a closed shop; and the offer of public money to finance postal ballots for union elections and other important union issues.

In the early stages of the election campaign, Margaret Thatcher and Jim Prior continued to give the subject their own quite different emphasis. On 8 April, on radio and television, Prior emphasised that the law only had a limited role to play in Tory plans for the trade unions, in specific areas like secondary picketing. At her opening press conference and at her own constituency adoption meeting at Finchley on 11 April, Mrs Thatcher said roundly, 'We shall not wait till there is another industrial crisis on our hands to bring about the changes that everyone knows are needed. I want to make it plain that the Conservative party will not turn back from these commitments.' She underlined the passage in the manifesto which proposed to ensure that the unions bore a fair share of the cost of supporting their members when on strike. The same day Prior was saying that a Conservative government would consult the unions on labour law reform, while only '. . . those changes which the unions recognise as necessary should be backed up by the force of law.'

For most of the next week, Mrs Thatcher continued to raise the spectre of union wreckers, asserting that her government would ensure that 'power and responsibility in future marched together'. Meanwhile Prior was hoping that *limited* changes in the law would galvanise moderate trade unionists into action. Indeed, trade union leaders at the TUC, watching the campaign with close interest, got the impression that Margaret Thatcher had made a deliberate decision to work the anti-union theme on a rising crescendo until polling day. Jim Prior shared this view. He was telling people at this time that, while he had won his battle for the manifesto, he had lost his war to stop a Conservative government rushing head-on into another clash with the unions. He assumed that Mrs Thatcher would only have him in her Cabinet as Minister of Employment if she was elected with the barest of majorities and needed all the support she could get. With a solid working majority, he was certain that she would set off without him on her much more radical policies.

Suddenly, however, with just over ten days to the election, Mrs Thatcher's whole campaign changed. In the last week her references to trade unions were muted, her chosen themes a more general concern for an expanding economy and a freer society. The reason for this switch was tactical. Going into the election campaign and despite the events of the winter, 'ability to handle the unions' was surprisingly the one issue on which Labour scored substantially higher than the Conservatives. An NOP opinion poll published on 6 April, for example, showed that only 35 per cent thought that the Tories would be better able to handle strikes, and only 19 per cent thought that Mrs Thatcher would be better at dealing with union leaders than Jim Callaghan. By the second week of the campaign, however, the private Tory tracking surveys showed that the position had changed. They were winning on the union issue. The same surveys, however, showed that Mrs Thatcher and the party were in danger of losing support on the grounds that they seemed too harsh and unfeeling, unable to understand traditional workers' solidarity. So the decision was taken to soft-pedal on the union issue.

The mood continued after the election. Jim Prior, to his surprise and despite Mrs Thatcher's majority, found himself at the Department of Employment. The only price was that the Prime Minister refused to allow Barney Hayhoe, the former Heath supporter who had been part of Prior's shadow employment team, to join him as his Minister of State. Instead, to his great annoyance, Hayhoe was offered a job as junior minister for the army. Prior was given a peer, Lord Gowrie, as his number two and Patrick Mayhew, a lawyer and a Thatcher supporter, as a junior minister. The appointment of Prior himself was an early example of Margaret Thatcher's political caution. To give him that job was the unradical, the safe, the expected thing to do. But she must have known, from her experience with him in the Shadow Cabinet, that as long as he was there, her government would not put through anything like the reform of trade union law that large numbers of those who voted for her expected.

The practical argument within the Conservative party focused on a number of detailed issues concerned with shifting the balance of power in industrial disputes away from organised labour and back towards managements. The debate concentrated on the question of whether or not to go back to the main provisions of Heath's 1971 Industrial Relations Act, which Labour had in effect repealed; whether to make unions liable at law for any actions of their members, acting officially or unofficially; whether to cut off Social Security benefits to the members of strikers' families; whether to change the PAYE income tax system which gives substantial and immediate tax rebates to strikers. There was also the whole range of questions about whether and how far to limit the near-total immunity from civil law granted by the 1974 and 1976 Labour trade union acts. The clear impression given by Mrs Thatcher before the election was that she personally favoured full implementation of such a programme. Her taxation adviser, Lord Cockfield, was particularly persuaded of the arguments in favour of withholding PAYE rebates.

Before the election Margaret Thatcher's formal contacts with the trade union movement had been negligible. She had one meeting over drinks in 1977 with the so-called Neddy six, the six trade union members of the National Economic Development Council (at the time only Len Murray, Jack Jones, Hugh Scanlon, Alf Allen and David Basnett, for Dan McGarvey had just died). The union side remembers that meeting as 'a total failure'. Mrs Thatcher gave them the impression that she neither understood the problems of trying to run the trade union movement, nor wanted to learn. Much of the time was taken up with argument between Keith Joseph and Jim Prior.

Afterwards, the TUC told Prior that they would like to try for another more constructive meeting, but it came to nothing. Further discussions between the future government and the trade union movement were conducted mainly with Jim Prior, Barney Hayhoe and Peter Walker, none of them close confidants of the Leader.

Mrs Thatcher met individual trade union leaders for discussion before the election, sometimes with, quite often without, Jim Prior. She communicated to most of them a dogmatic belief in the efficiency of a properly functioning free market, a world in which the contribution of unions at best was minimal and at worst seriously obstructive. In such a free market economy the only substantial function of trade unionists was to negotiate hard for the best wages and conditions of service that each employer could afford. It was certainly no part of their business to be drawn into the process of running the country.

Such also was the message from her first meeting with the TUC as Prime Minister, which took place at their request at No. 10 on 25 June. The TUC team was from its important economic committee, led by Lord Allen, president of the shopworkers' union, USDAW. It included Len Murray, Clive Jenkins of ASTMS, Moss Evans of the Transport and General, Joe Gormley of the miners, Terry Duffy of the AUEW and Tom Jackson of the Post Office workers.

The meeting was a disaster from the start. Although Len Murray had spent an hour with Mrs Thatcher in advance, the TUC team adopted the wrong tactics. They came with an agenda in their minds that was far too wide for a first meeting, covering virtually the whole of government–trade union relations. They had agreed in advance that the speaking from their side would be done only by Lord Allen and Len Murray. Allen opened by saying that he assumed the Prime Minister would like to know why the TUC had asked for the meeting. Mrs Thatcher said yes, but before allowing Lord Allen to speak, herself launched into a very prolonged opening monologue. Her remarks provoked Duffy and Jackson into breaking ranks and speaking out of turn. Jim Prior, sitting on one side of the Prime Minister, said nothing and looked glum throughout. Sir Geoffrey Howe on the other side spoke only in answer to direct questions from her. Gormley, with Yorkshire directness, refused point blank to answer her questions, on the grounds that he had agreed in advance not to speak. The meeting broke up in a shambles.

From the end of June at least until February, when all the old sores were re-opened by the mass picketing and other events associated with the steel strike, Jim Prior became visibly more assured that his minimalist reform postion was holding the day. His public performances, particularly at the monthly meetings of Neddy, became more obviously confident. There seemed also during the year to be a gradual change in the Prime Minister's own attitude to the need to keep up some continuing dialogue with the unions.

The first test had been what she would decide to do about Neddy itself. This body had been set up by Selwyn Lloyd when he was Chancellor in 1962, as part of a policy to improve the performance of the British economy. But its constitution and purpose contradict the main part of Joseph's economic philosophy.

For Neddy says, by its very existence, that the operations of the free market are producing an unsatisfactorily poor performance, which should be improved by the government, employers and the unions getting together outside the framework of Parliament and Whitehall to try to do better. There was, therefore, a real possibility that Mrs Thatcher would abolish it, or at least substantially reduce its status.

Sir Keith Joseph might have been inclined to go the whole hog. Others persuaded the Prime Minister to let it continue, while reviewing the usefulness of some of its less effective activities in particular industrial sectors. Howe saw merit in Neddy as a forum where more open and informed discussion of the state of the economy and of the government's objectives could take place. The late Sir John Methven, director general of the CBI and a man who had the Prime Minister's ear, was strongly in favour of keeping Neddy. Like Len Murray, he was concerned to preserve for future use as much as possible of the web of relationships between the CBI, the TUC and government.

In the event Neddy was left untouched. The only threat to it came, as it were, from the other direction. For a while in November, it looked as if the trade unionists might boycott its proceedings in protest against the government's treatment of the NEB over Rolls-Royce. In particular, David Basnett of the General and Municipal Worker's Union, who had been on the NEB which resigned *en masse*, took some cooling down, before he agreed to continue working with Neddy.

By the time she went to Blackpool in October for her first Conservative party conference as Prime Minister, Mrs Thatcher seemed positively to be holding out a public olive branch to the unions. Though she made it clear in her speech that the government would introduce a bill before the end of the year, designed to strike a 'fair balance between a man's right to withhold his labour and a small minority's determination to impose its will upon the majority', she wanted 'free and responsible trade unions to play an honourable part in the life of a free and responsible society'. Her speech included these words: 'I give them my pledge that, however often we may be rebuffed, my colleagues and I will continue to talk to them, to listen to their views, and to give those views due weight in shaping national policy, so long as it is understood that national policy is in the last resort the sole responsibility of government and Parliament.' By

January, when the Prime Minister took the chair for the first time at
a monthly Neddy meeting, although the steel strike was already
under way, her message to the unions was of the need for co-
operation and understanding. She seemed, as one of them remarked,
like a changed woman.

The state of the tactical battle within the Cabinet on the issue of
trade union law reform was duly reflected in the Employment Bill
that Jim Prior presented to Parliament in December. It had been
drawn up as the result of almost daily consultation between Prior and
Harry Urwin, deputy general-secretary of the Transport and
General Workers who was representing the TUC. Prior used the
fruits of this consultation as ammunition against his more radical
colleagues in the Cabinet. The bill proposed the minimum that was
consistent with the manifesto, perhaps even rather less. It offered
some improvement in the lot of those who fell foul of closed shops. It
promised financial support for union ballots. It proposed a right of
appeal to the High Court against unfair exclusion from union
membership. And it contained provisions that would allow
employers to apply for injunctions against secondary picketing of
their premises, if these were not directly involved in a dispute. It said
nothing, however, about secondary, or sympathy, *strikes*. Prior was
clearly in charge.

There remained, however, a strong minority in the Cabinet,
including the Prime Minister, Howe and Joseph, but not on this
issue Biffen, who were shocked by Prior's rigid refusal to move faster
and further. In their view, he was obsessed by the 1970–74 Heath
government's defeats in its legal and industrial wrangles with the
unions and blind to the changed mood of the country. His unargued
assertions in the Shadow Cabinet that he alone knew what was and
was not possible with the unions had infuriated them, particularly Sir
Geoffrey Howe, who as Solicitor General had been one of the main
architects of the 1971 Industrial Relations Act. They were now
increasingly convinced that a golden political opportunity was being
missed.

In these arguments, and as the Employment Bill wound its way
through Parliament, there was a scale against which it was possible to
measure where the running tug-of-war between the hawks and the
doves was standing at any moment. True 'wets' wished to go no
further than the position set out in the published bill. When Len

Murray and others attacked these proposals as an unacceptable assault on the fundamental rights of the British working man, the rhetoric was designed to conceal surprise that the government was only proposing to go thus far, and to discourage it from going any further. At this stage, the TUC was hoping that it would be possible to get bi-partisan legislation, taking trade union law out of politics at least for a while.

The rising scale of possible further action went as follows: first, a quick, short bill dealing just with the issue of secondary picketing; second, legislation to deal with sympathy strikes; third, restriction of the immunities of trade unions, or individuals engaged in union activity; and finally, at the top of the scale, legislation making unions legally responsible for all the actions of their members, combined with a right of recourse to union funds for those claiming civil damages. This last would have been seen by the union movement as an outright declaration of war.

Until the turn of the year, Jim Prior might have been forgiven for being pleased at the success of his stalling tactics. The only question was whether such a mouse of a bill was worth the ritual song and dance that it was bound to provoke. Then, however, he was almost overwhelmed by the consequences of two events. The first was a series of judgments by the judges of the House of Lords. The second was the steel strike. They reminded everyone unavoidably that, despite what Margaret Thatcher had said in the election campaign, another industrial crisis was on their hands and 'the changes that everyone knows are needed' were neither enacted, nor even in the bill before Parliament.

The government and Jim Prior had been praying that the thorny question of secondary blacking, or sympathetic strikes, had been solved for them by Lord Denning and the Court of Appeal. The key case was known as *MacShane vs Express Newspapers Ltd.* It involved the National Union of Journalists, of which MacShane was president, calling out its members working for the Press Association news agency in support of a strike by provincial journalists against provincial newspaper owners, and then instructing journalists at the *Daily Express* to black any of the agency copy produced by the PA. The appeal court had held that the action at the *Daily Express* was so far removed from the actual dispute that it was no longer covered by the total civil immunity given by the 1974 and 1976 Acts to any action properly taken 'in furtherance of a trade dispute'.

But this was not to remain the position for long. On 13 December all five judges of the House of Lords announced their finding that Lord Denning and his colleagues had read a limitation into Section 13 of the 1974 Act that its wording simply did not bear. The intention of Parliament at that time had been clear. It wished to give the widest possible immunity to trade unions from civil actions. If the present government wanted the law to be different, it would have to change it.

Even so, Mrs Thatcher appeared to remain quite relaxed on the subject. As late as 6 January, for example, she gave a television interview to Brian Walden on *Weekend World*. Most of it was concerned with trade unions. She was happy to describe the Employment Bill as 'modest and sensible'. She gave a clear hint that, because of the need for consultation and 'time to get it right', the secondary strike problem created by the MacShane judgment would not be dealt with in the present bill, but in later legislation. She said only that the government was 'thinking of looking' at the civil immunities of trade unions, where they were involved in breach of commercial contracts. She ruled out the possibility of making strikes illegal in certain essential public services. She said that the government was 'not very enamoured at the moment' of the idea that people on strike should have their Social Security benefits reduced by an amount that their union would be 'deemed' to have paid them in strike pay, whether it had or not.

As January wore on, however, the public and political reaction to the secondary picketing of private steel companies forced her to think again. Prior announced on 30 January that new proposals on secondary strike action would be put into the Employment Bill during its committee stage. The aim would be to make the law what Lord Denning had interpreted it as in the MacShane case. He insisted, however, that there would be ample time for consultation with the unions. The next day, despite strong rumblings within her party because the main steel union was not paying strike pay to its members, the Prime Minister said in the House of Commons that the government had no plans to force unions to do so.

Serious pressure was now building up on the Cabinet. On 1 February the House of Lords threw out an injunction that Duport Steel and 15 other private steel companies had obtained the previous week from Lord Denning's Court of Appeal, granted in open defiance of the previous MacShane ruling in the Lords. That injunction had ordered the steel union to stop its secondary strikes against the private sector firms.

The battle inside the Cabinet in the following week was between those who wanted to include clauses on picketing and trade union immunities immediately in the existing bill and those who refused to be rushed. Sir John Methven of the CBI, normally a Prior supporter, broke ranks over the week-end and called for profound changes in the law to 'bring sanity back to industrial relations'. This contrasted starkly with Prior saying on BBC radio that, if the government got its industrial policy wrong again this time round 'the outlook for the country is very bleak indeed', and Len Murray for the TUC saying that 'if there is a full frontal attack on trade union rights, there will be a full frontal defence by the trade union movement.' Following an irate exchange with Prior, Methven re-joined the moderates in a speech to the National Federation of Building Trades Employers on 9 February when he said: 'We could have a disaster on our hands if we try in the present frenzied atmosphere to put hasty legislation on the statute book without proper consultation.'

The steel strike was now causing further strain within the Cabinet. Sir Keith Joseph, with his responsibility for the government's policy of inaction in the steel dispute, took the view that it was 'deplorable . . . that the law should allow the private steel sector – where there is no quarrel between the employers and the unions – to be drawn into this dispute'. He added pointedly that this was a matter for the employment secretary (House of Commons, 4 February). Jim Prior, in contrast, was taking the view that the incompetent handling of the steel dispute was suddenly putting at risk his efforts 'to make changes which will last this country 15 or 20 years and put it back in a proper industrial position where everyone can prosper' (House of Commons standing committee on the Employment Bill, 5 February). During February, Prior became involved in private initiatives to bring the two sides in the steel dispute together, which came to nothing. As a result, his authority with his colleagues suffered somewhat for a time.

At this moment, events at Hadfields, a private Sheffield steel company owned by Lonrho, substantially heightened the drama. Its Sheffield works had been subjected to increasingly violent picketing, but work had continued. At the end of the first week in February, the local Assistant Chief Constable told the managing director that, given the mood of the pickets outside, he could no longer guarantee the physical security of the plant and machinery inside. Faced with that advice Hadfields closed down, the pickets claiming a triumphant victory.

The incident was not reported, but on the following Tuesday, 5 February, the managing director, Derek Norton, came down to London for a well publicised confrontation with Sir Charles Villiers, chairman of the BSC. He also saw privately Ian Gow, the Prime Minister's Parliamentary Private Secretary, who conveyed the story of the Sheffield incident to the Prime Minister. The same day she spent an hour with a delegation of private steel manufacturers, who waved her own election manifesto in front of her and demanded without much finesse to know when her government was going to fulfil its commitments to protect them from secondary strikes.

Meanwhile the Conservative press was concertedly calling for blood, *Daily Telegraph* leaders in particular. 'It may be no exaggeration to say that the coming week will seal the fate of the Thatcher administration,' said the paper. Four days later it was of the opinion that a handful of resignations might be preferable to the catastrophe of Mrs Thatcher hesitating much longer and 'dissipating the country's resolve for firm action'. The *Daily Express* in the same tone told the Prime Minister, 'If you don't act now the writing will be on the tombstone of the Tory Government.'

There was also now parliamentary pressure on Prior. On 4 February nearly 100 Conservative MPs put their names to an early day motion, calling for immediate legislation to restore industrial equity. He decided to face the demands directly and, with the co-operation of its chairman, Edward Du Cann, spoke to a crowded meeting of the 1922 Committee on Thursday, 7 February. It was described by one person present as 'a bravura performance'. He conceded little and demonstrated that most of his critics had no grasp of what the subject entailed. He said that his bill would be on the statute book by August, well in time for the next autumn's round of industrial action. He hinted that other matters might be taken up in subsequent legislation, and that the question of cutting Social Security payments to strikers' families was under consideration. By the end of the meeting Prior had persuaded the majority of his party that to legislate hastily when tempers were so high and without adequate consultation would only make things worse.

The 1922 Committee still refuses to allow its officers to talk about its affairs to journalists. A brief was however given to Derek Howe, the government's political press secretary, who spoke to lobby correspondents. The accounts of the meeting that appeared the next day only served to increase the sense of frustration felt by the Prime Minister and the other radicals at Prior's success in blocking their attempts to get more rapid change. The fact was that they did not have a majority for what they wanted, either in the Cabinet itself, or the Cabinet committee E which was dealing with the bill, where Whitelaw, Walker, Biffen and Lord Hailsham all ranged with Prior. Mrs Thatcher failed at this stage to get her colleagues to agree to a quick one-clause bill to put the secondary picketing provisions of the existing bill onto the statute book at once. Much to the annoyance of Du Cann and those who had arranged the 1922 Committee meeting, Sir Geoffrey Howe now gave public vent to this frustration, though he had said little in Cabinet, in a speech that week-end at Taunton. It was prepared with the help of the No. 10 policy unit and with the active encouragement of the Prime Minister herself.

His hard line was that the existing bill was inadequate. A long programme of reform in industrial law was needed. 'It would be fatal to Britain's chances, if this government lost its nerve and neglected its clear duty to take in hand the necessary reform of the law.' It was a clear attempt to create a climate of opinion which would force the government into committing itself to more trade union legislation after the present minimal bill had been swallowed.

The Prime Minister in her frustration also decided to attack. At Question Time in the House of Commons on Thursday, 14 February, she announced, claiming wrongly that the specific proposal had been in the manifesto, that plans were going ahead for a scheme whereby certain amounts from union funds would be 'deemed' to have been paid to strikers, whether they had or not, and then deducted from Social Security payments to them. She hoped to be in a position to make an announcement soon. This was the very scheme that she had 'not been very enamoured of' on *Weekend World* in January. Jim Prior was surprised and angry, for there had been no Cabinet decision on the subject. She had reverted to her habit of making policy by personal assertion. It rapidly became clear that the idea bristled with difficulties to which solutions had by no means been found.

A central problem was how to put pressure on unions to give strike pay to members without being grossly unfair to non-unionists who became involved in strikes. As Mrs Thatcher had said to Brian Walden, you cannot deem non-trade-union members to have had strike pay that they could not possibly have had. There was also bound to be difficulty over distinctions between official and unofficial strikes. On 26 March, when he presented his second budget, Sir Geoffrey Howe announced the government's conclusion that £12 a week should be docked from any supplementary benefit paid to a striker's family, regardless of whether he or she belonged to a union. The change could not come into force without new legislation. It remained to be seen precisely how the practical problems would be handled.

For a while thereafter, attention was diverted from Prior's bill by the issue of criminal, as opposed to civil, law. Lord Hailsham in a speech to a Young Conservatives conference said that the 'appalling scenes' outside Hadfields in Sheffield were in his view clear breaches of the criminal law. Such a statement by the Lord Chancellor himself invited questions about what the government proposed to do. Did the criminal law need strengthening? Were the police doing their duty? The matter was urgent, because there was about to be further serious confrontation with mass pickets at another private steel works at Sheerness in Kent.

Sir Michael Havers, the Attorney General, duly made a statement to the House on 19 February. His message was a surprising anti-climax. The government had found that the police had all the powers they needed under the Public Order Act, the Criminal Law Act, several other statutes and indeed under common law to deal with what was happening, but were not, it seemed, prepared to use these powers fully. The rising head of steam within the Conservative party on this issue, including demands that the law should be changed to limit the number of those who could legally man a picket line, quickly evaporated when the police also made clear their view that the criminal law did not require strengthening, and that they were reluctant to become further involved in disputes, because then they would seem to lose their impartiality by siding with employers against workers.

In the Cabinet battle about secondary strikes, meanwhile, Prior continued to hold his ground. When after much delay the Cabinet agreed a working paper for discussion with the TUC and the CBI, it was clear that Mrs Thatcher and Sir Geoffrey Howe had not carried any major points. The previous government's Acts taken together had removed all common law rights to sue for damages where a trade union was taking action 'in contemplation or furtherance of a trade dispute'. Prior now proposed that two new tests should be applied in order that unions should in future qualify for that immunity. First, what a union did must be reasonably *capable* of furthering the dispute in question. Second, the industrial action must be 'predominantly in pursuit' of a trade dispute and not for some extraneous motive. In practice these two new tests of capability and motive would only withdraw immunity from an obviously political strike. They would have done little to change the position in relation to sympathy strikes in the private steel industry, for these were clearly capable of influencing the main trade dispute between the steel unions and the BSC. The Prior proposals contained one other cosmetic change. In future, anybody other than a direct customer or supplier of the firm involved in a strike would have protection through the courts against breach of commercial contracts, though still not against unions inducing their work force to break contracts of employment.

Not without reason, Prior felt that he had won the long battle handsomely on points. After the working paper was published he was attacked, when he appeared before the House of Commons select committee on employment, for cowardice in the face of trade union blackmail. With rising voice and deepening colour, he declared that it might be easier to be tougher than he was proposing to be with the unions, but it would do the country no good to be led into civil disobedience and further strikes. 'Sometimes it requires courage to stand against the stream. I believe I am standing against the stream', he shouted.

Once again the Prime Minister used television where she could not get her way in Cabinet. Deciding at short notice to give an interview to BBC's *Panorama*, she made it clear in answer to questions from Robin Day that, if things did not work after the Prior bill, the government would re-open the question of immunity of union funds from claims for damages. This had been considered by the Cabinet and rejected on the grounds that it would put part of trade union law back substantially to what it had been before the basic Trade Disputes Act of 1906.

Now Mrs Thatcher said that this question was still an open one. She was deliberately breaking the convention that members of a government must individually support in public decisions collectively reached in Cabinet. She was doing so because, like Robin Day on the air, her supporters were reminding her that the election manifesto nine months before had said that a Conservative government would 'ensure that the protection of the law is available to those not concerned in [a] dispute but who at present can suffer severely from secondary action'. Her object, she said, was to do just that and 'by the time the next election is here we've got to have done it'. February 1980 was clearly not going to be the last battle that Margaret Thatcher and Jim Prior would have on trade union reform.

The right wing of the party continued to harass Prior in Parliament as the bill went through committee. They forced votes against the government in April on making union funds available to compensate for loss from secondary picketing and on limiting the closed shop. On 22 April they staged the biggest revolt of Mrs Thatcher's first year, when 45 Conservative back-benchers voted against the government for an amendment that would have obliged a union to hold a secret ballot if 15 per cent or 500 of its members called for one. On all these votes the government was in no danger, because the Labour Opposition voted with them. The rebels were making it clear beyond doubt, however, that the argument was not settled and would be carried forward to the party conference in the autumn.

Chapter 5

Certainly no one need expect me or m
to be backward in defence of Britain's

Mrs Thatcher, giving the Winston Churchill Memorial Lecture in Luxembourg on 18 October, 1979.

PRESIDENTS, PRIME MINISTERS AND ex-Prime Ministers are prone to find foreign affairs and the international stage a seductive escape from the more tawdry realities of domestic politics. It is seldom, however, that these matters influence or excite the great British public. Margaret Thatcher's first year was something of an exception. Rhodesia, Vietnamese boat people, the European reaction to revolution in Iran and to the Soviet invasion of Afghanistan, a possible boycott of the Moscow Olympics, a major confrontation with the EEC over the budget – day after day all these issues were front page news in our normally parochial newspapers. On all of them Margaret Thatcher, her Foreign Secretary, Lord Carrington, and other ministers were actively and visibly involved. More than that, in a year when on the economic and industrial front there seemed to be a stubborn lack of progress, the main successes of the year were in the foreign field. Certainly, Lord Carrington must be judged to be the Cabinet minister who most substantially increased his reputation during the year. To find the last time that had happened to an incumbent of the Foreign Office one would probably have to go back to Ernie Bevin, the foundation of the North Atlantic Treaty Organisation and the Berlin airlift of 1948.

Margaret Thatcher was, of modern Prime Ministers, uniquely inexperienced in matters of foreign policy and the arts of diplomacy. Even a hagiographer like Russell Lewis was forced to write of her, 'Her interest in foreign affairs has not been marked, but that is perhaps no bad thing.'

On becoming Leader of the Opposition in 1975, Margaret Thatcher knew that this was a deficiency that a potential Prime Minister needed to repair. She set off on the standard round of visits to foreign capitals. She also devoted time to thinking what her attitude should be towards the Soviet Union, on questions of western defence, on the Atlantic Alliance. She consulted widely, using in particular the Centre for Policy Studies as a source of ideas. She came to value the contributions of people like Professor Hugh Thomas. She began to make substantial and elegantly phrased speeches on international themes. The most celebrated was delivered in Kensington town hall in January 1976. Its theme was that the Soviet Union was bent on world dominance. Its slogan was that Britain must awake. The greater part of the speech was devoted to defence. The continuing increase in Soviet defence budgets proved that the Russians were not genuinely interested in détente. This constituted a threat to Britain and other western countries that must be met by increasing our own preparedness. The speech was so notably aggressive in tone and content that the Soviet Ambassador in London was instructed three days later to complain formally to the Foreign Office about it. This speech led *Red Star*, the Soviet defence ministry newspaper, to dub her the next day 'the iron lady', who was bent on destroying east-west détente. It was a sobriquet that did not upset her in her quest for the right electoral image. In 1977 she had her first meeting with President Carter in the White House. In her eagerness, she did so much of the talking that Carter was forced, towards the end of the allotted time, to ask whether there was anything *she* wanted to learn from *him*.

On the critical issue of Europe and the referendum on Labour's renegotiated terms for membership of the Common Market, she campaigned and voted in favour of continued participation. But she did so without zeal. Indeed, right up to the election itself, while always using the correct formal words about 'the Tory party's whole-hearted commitment to the success of the Community', she nevertheless always contrived to give the impression that, at the very least, she had severe reservations about most of its central policies.

Rhodesia, however, was to be by far the most surprising foreign policy episode of Margaret Thatcher's first year. In the course of it, she achieved such a total reversal of policy that even the pro-Rhodesian lobby within her own party could not believe what was happening until it was too late for them to do anything about it.

During the election campaign Mrs Thatcher managed to avoid saying much on the subject. The white voters of Rhodesia had by referendum overwhelmingly endorsed the introduction of a new constitution, based for the first time on black majority rule. As a result of elections held under this new constitution, Bishop Abel Muzorewa had become the first black Prime Minister of Rhodesia on 24 April, 1979. The Conservatives had sent a team of observers, led by Lord Boyd, a former Colonial Secretary, to observe these elections and to report whether they were 'free and fair'. For as the shadow Foreign Secretary, Francis Pym, said early in the British election campaign, if it was established that the Rhodesian elections had taken place in 'reasonably free and fair conditions', then the last of the long established 'six principles' for recognising the end of the 1965 'rebellion' in Rhodesia would have been met.

Lord Boyd, when he returned to London with his team after 24 April, was actively discouraged from rushing out his report and presenting it to the party leader, though in fact its substance was soon ready and his conclusions both predictable and predicted. It was not formally presented until 16 May, two weeks after the election. Until that point, Mrs Thatcher was able to say that she was waiting for the Boyd report, before committing herself to any specific action. From that point onward, however, the general expectation grew rapidly that economic sanctions against Rhodesia would be lifted and the new régime recognised. This was not the policy of Lord Carrington and the Foreign Office, though they had long realised that it would be difficult to stop the bandwagon, particularly since it seemed to have the Prime Minister firmly aboard it. Even before the election, on a visit to Washington, Carrington had told the Americans that an incoming Tory government would find it politically impossible to renew the economic sanctions against Rhodesia for another year, 'even if the Archangel Gabriel came down to argue for them'.

Matters came to a head with a press conference given by Mrs Thatcher in Canberra, when she stopped off on her way back from her first western economic summit meeting in Tokyo at the end of June. In long discussions with the Australians, Malcolm Fraser, the Prime Minister, and Andrew Peacock, the Minister for Foreign Affairs, Mrs Thatcher failed to persuade them to take a more positive view of the Muzorewa régime in Salisbury. Fraser, who is something of a political hero to Margaret Thatcher, tried to persuade her not to meet the press. Her last few days had been tiring and he knew that Australian journalists, most of them unsympathetic to white Rhodesia, might give her a rough ride. But she insisted.

Reports of that week-end press conference in the British papers on 2 July caused a minor sensation. Though there was nothing like a verbatim text anywhere, she was reported to have said that she doubted very much whether renewal of sanctions could be got through Parliament again; that, apart from the lifting of sanctions, the recognition of the Muzorewa government was a separate issue, which might take 'just a little longer'; and that it would be wrong to be 'too pessimistic' about other governments joining Britain in a collective act of recognition of the Bishop's administration.

To anyone who knew Mrs Thatcher's private views, there was nothing very surprising in these statements. Once again, however, she seemed to be 'making policy on the hoof' on a delicate issue, this time while thousands of miles from home. Predictably, officials in Salisbury at once expressed their delight at this evidence that the British government was now moving in their direction. Lord Harlech, the government's special envoy to Southern Africa, was arriving in Rhodesia that very week.

For the Foreign Office and Lord Carrington the timing of her remarks was disastrous. The threats that sanctions might be continued and official recognition withheld were the only points at which pressure could be brought to bear on the Salisbury government to make changes in its constitution. In the Foreign Office view several aspects of the existing constitution were unacceptable. These included notably the entrenched blocking power over any change in the constitution which was given to the white minority members of parliament for a decade, and the extensive reserved rights of the civil service commissions to resist the promotion of blacks.

A rather sharp telegram was sent to the British High Commission in Canberra, asking for a full account of what the Prime Minister had actually said. The reply offered some little comfort. The contentious passages had not been in the Prime Minister's opening statement to the press conference, which had lasted for about 15 minutes. Contrary to Fraser's fears, this had ended with something like an ovation from the assembled journalists. It was after that, in a mood of some elation at the way things were going, that she had answered questions off the cuff and had made remarks which the journalists had reasonably interpreted. It was still clear, however, that the Prime Minister's performance had been deliberate. She had chosen to put down her marker, because she felt that Carrington and his officials were conspiring with the Americans to slide out of the manifesto commitments on Rhodesia. The manifesto had said that, provided the celebrated six principles were satisfied by the April election, a Tory government 'will have the duty to return Rhodesia to a state of legality, move to lift sanctions, and do its utmost to ensure that the new independent state gains international recognition'. Lord Boyd's report had given its seal of approval. Lord Home, who had invented the first five of the principles, agreed that they had been met. Harold Wilson, who had added the sixth, was in agreement. As she saw it, there was an unanswerable moral case for recognising the Salisbury government and no legal reason for denying it. Why was the Foreign Office back-sliding?

As a matter of parliamentary arithmetic, Margaret Thatcher was wrong to assert that a sanctions renewal order would have failed in Parliament. Certainly, there was a substantial group within the Tory party, perhaps as many as 80 centred in the right-wing Monday Club, that would have voted against the government on sanctions, however the policy was presented. On the other side, however, there was a significant group of back-benchers, known formally to the Whips as the A group, which would have supported the renewal of sanctions as part of a coherent policy. This group, previously organised by Neil Marten (until Mrs Thatcher made him the junior minister responsible for overseas aid), was now being led by Terence Higgins and Peter Emery. Indeed, later in the year, the leaders of this group called on Sir Ian Gilmour at the Foreign Office to persuade him that their votes, plus those of more than 100 MPs directly on the government's payroll, would give a sanctions renewal order a majority, even without Opposition votes. With Opposition votes an order would be overwhelmingly secure.

This is all speculation, for events were to turn out very differently. What is certain is that her off-the-cuff remarks in Canberra raised the expectations of the pro-Rhodesia lobby. As Winston Churchill was to say of this event in the House of Commons debate on Southern Africa at the end of the month, 'I believe that it was an expression of a considered opinion with which the overwhelming majority of Conservative members would agree.'

When Mrs Thatcher returned to Downing Street on 3 July, therefore, it would have taken an unusual clairvoyant to predict the events of the next eight months in Zimbabwe-Rhodesia, as the country had become under its new constitution a month earlier. The idea that a Thatcher government would, as one of Britain's last major colonial acts, restore legality and then grant independence to Rhodesia had always been a strong possibility. But the idea that this transfer of legitimate power would be to a self-proclaimed Marxist, Robert Mugabe, whom Mrs Thatcher herself had been calling a terrorist and 'no better than the IRA' in May, was pure fantasy. The further possibility that such a development would be seen as a triumph for Mrs Thatcher's government and for Lord Carrington personally, would have been an even more ridiculous proposition.

It has been suggested that Mrs Thatcher's conversion took place at the Commonwealth heads of government meeting in Lusaka at the beginning of August. Some would have it that Margaret Thatcher received there her first education into the realities of African politics, or that she changed her mind because she got carried away by the conference itself. Others would have it that Lord Carrington, using the atmosphere and the evidence of Lusaka, was able to convince her of the necessity of changing to the policy that, in the end, led through the Lancaster House conference to the political annihilation of Bishop Muzorewa and Ian Smith and the election of Robert Mugabe as Prime Minister. Neither of these versions is true.

Margaret Thatcher's essential conversion on Rhodesia took place at the beginning of July, almost as soon as she got off the aeroplane from Canberra. Lord Carrington and his Foreign Office officials prepared a paper, which was waiting for her on her return. It said, quite simply, that the position she had adopted in Canberra was wrong. If she maintained it, it would be disastrous to the interests of the west in general and Britain in particular. The policy must be changed. The arguments were presented persuasively and Mrs Thatcher accepted them then and there.

They were the arguments of *realpolitik*. The position of the Foreign Office remained the same as it had been under the previous government. Western power and influence must not continue to be thrown into propping up white minority governments that would sooner rather than later be swept aside by nationalist movements, as in Angola and Mozambique, nor in supporting corrupt and unpopular black régimes, as elsewhere in Africa. The capacity of the Soviet Union and its satellites, for example Cuba and East Germany, to influence events in Africa had in the past been hugely increased by working with genuine and successful nationalist movements and not against them.

In Rhodesia, the inevitable outcome after more years of increasingly bitter guerilla war would be an eventual victory for the Patriotic Front under Joshua Nkomo and Robert Mugabe. To recognise the Muzorewa régime would imply a moral commitment to provide him with the military and economic support required to fight off the Patriotic Front. Troops might have to be sent in against the guerillas, at least to evacuate the white population. The Americans would not support such a policy, which they would see as playing directly into the hands of the Soviet Union. Indeed, in July President Carter announced that the United States would maintain economic sanctions against Zimbabwe-Rhodesia, since the recent elections had been 'neither fair nor free'. Unilateral British action would, therefore, involve a public split with the United States, damaging the political influence of the Atlantic Alliance. For what it mattered, such action would be a breach of the United Kingdom's obligation to the United Nations. Retaliation against Britain's far more extensive commercial interests elsewhere in black Africa, particularly in Nigeria, would be inevitable and serious. In addition, on close study, the existing constitution was unworkable and unacceptable.

In short, the Foreign Office argued, the question that Lord Boyd and his observers had asked was irrelevant. It mattered not whether the election under the recently introduced constitution had been conducted freely and fairly. In a technical sense and within the limits of an African country in a state of civil war, that condition had been met. The only relevant question was whether the constitution itself was one which had any hope of providing Rhodesia with a serious chance of ending the civil war and moving to independence under a stable and popular black government. The answer to that question was emphatically no.

It is curious that Mrs Thatcher's complete acceptance of these arguments went unnoticed before she flew off to the Commonwealth conference in Lusaka on 30 July. This was despite the fact that in opening an adjournment debate in the House of Commons on the previous Wednesday, 25 July, she gave the clearest indications that her views had changed. In her speech she rehearsed the history of Rhodesia since the illegal declaration of independence in 1965. She ran over the six principles which previous governments had established as the test for a return to normality. She recognised the historic advance implied by the new constitution and the holding of the first elections ever in Rhodesia on the basis of universal suffrage. She paid tribute to Lord Boyd and his report. From that point on, however, she departed totally from her previous position.

The manifesto had said that, if the necessary conditions were met, a Tory government would return Rhodesia to a state of legality and *do its utmost* to ensure that it gained international recognition. Mrs Thatcher now said that British government policy was based on finding a solution which met the 'democratic wishes of the people of Rhodesia' *and which ensured* that the new legal and independent country gained international recognition. The changed wording was not an accident. A new requirement was being added, over and above the fulfilment of the old six principles. 'At the same time,' she said, 'because it is in Rhodesia's own interest to be accepted fully into the international community, we must have regard to the views of other governments.' She made it clear that by this she meant the views of the 'front-line' states bordering on Rhodesia, that is Tanzania, Zambia, Botswana, Angola and Mozambique, as well as those of other black African countries like Nigeria and Malawi.

Mrs Thatcher even refused to say whether she endorsed Lord Boyd's judgment that the April elections had been an acceptable expression of the will of the Rhodesian people. Her words were unambiguous. 'That was his view. We have not yet decided on the matter, because we have wanted to go another way – a way that we believe will be better for Rhodesia in the longer run. It is a way that we believe will bring more countries along with us, and if we go along that consultation route it will be to the benefit of Rhodesia.'

The whole game was to be played again on a new pitch. She and Lord Carrington were going to Lusaka for consultations with the Commonwealth. Only after that would the government put forward proposals on the constitutional arrangements by which legal independence for Rhodesia might be achieved. It was clear that no solution based on the existing constitution would now be acceptable.

Looking back on that debate in the light of subsequent events, it is extraordinary that the significance of what Mrs Thatcher had said escaped almost everyone. The government, of course, had no motive for giving publicity to a change of policy that would be repugnant to a large number of its own back-benchers. As it happened, neither Hansard nor *The Times*'s parliamentary report was appearing at the time because of industrial disputes. It is, however, a comment on the inadequacy of the reporting of Parliament that Mrs Thatcher could fly off to Lusaka at the beginning of the following week with so little notice having been taken of such a substantial shift in her position.

The orchestrated campaign against her in black Africa as she arrived in Zambia was violent. In advance of the Commonwealth meeting, for the first time in a year, the five front-line Presidents had come together in Lusaka. This was part of President Kenneth Kaunda's campaign to preserve a united front against what he thought was Margaret Thatcher's 'creeping recognition' of the Muzorewa régime. The pro-government *Times of Zambia* carried a banner headline on the eve of her arrival, proclaiming 'KK lashes Thatcher'. The Lagos government nationalised the Nigerian assets of BP on 31 July, the timing obviously designed to co-incide with Lusaka.

On the flight to Zambia, Lord Carrington, sitting behind the Prime Minister, noticed that she had two pairs of big dark glasses in her handbag. 'It's in case they get rough and start throwing anything like acid', she told him. When the plane had come to a halt outside the Lusaka airport terminal building, the doors opened and at once they were engulfed by a hot African night and a pandemonium of crowds, struggling journalists, photographers and television crews. Mrs Thatcher rose from her seat and walked without hesitation, or backward glance, straight down the steps and into the *mêlée*. Carrington was impressed.

The Lusaka conference became a triumph for Margaret Thatcher. To the astonishment of those closely involved, having totally switched her own position, Mrs Thatcher now became an even greater enthusiast for a settlement involving the Patriotic Front than Lord Carrington himself. Before Lusaka and during the subsequent Lancaster House conference, the Foreign Secretary had a clear strategic aim. He doubted whether it would ever be possible to come to a satisfactory negotiated deal with Robert Mugabe and

Joshua Nkomo. He was determined, however, to be sufficiently sympathetic to black African sentiments to separate the Patriotic Front from their sponsors, the Presidents of the five neighbouring front-line states.

The Rhodesian bush war was a crippling burden to their own economies. Zambia particularly had suffered as a result of 15 years of economic sanctions against Rhodesia. Being forced to play host to revolutionary guerilla armies caused internal political problems for the governments of Zambia and Mozambique and military embarrassment whenever their bases were subject to periodic reprisals by the Rhodesian armed forces. If the Muzorewa régime could be forced to accept enough of the constitutional changes regarded as essential by figures like Machel of Mozambique, Nyerere of Tanzania, or Kaunda of Zambia, they might decide that it was politically possible to withdraw support from the guerillas.

Mrs Thatcher, however, now took a more advanced view than Carrington. If the argument was that, for once, Britain and the west should try not to be on the losing side in a colonial war against a nationalist movement, then we had better make a serious effort to come to terms with the Patriotic Front. At Lusaka, Carrington several times thought that the point had come where there was no further sense in trying to reach negotiated agreement with the whole Commonwealth. The main credit for persevering with the ultimately successful proposals for the Lancaster House conference goes to Margaret Thatcher and Sir Sonny Ramphal, the Commonwealth Secretary-General. It was Mrs Thatcher who chided Carrington for being excessively cynical about the reliability of the word of this or that African President. Almost until the end of the Lancaster House conference in December, Carrington was prepared to take bets that the Patriotic Front would not sign an agreement.

Mrs Thatcher, too, was willing to take greater risks for a Rhodesia settlement than any British government since 1965. For example, she accepted the very substantial risks involved in putting British commanded troops into Rhodesia to monitor the ceasefire. No British government in the previous 15 years had dared to contemplate putting British troops into a position where they might have to fight, even if only in self-defence, against either the Rhodesian armed forces or the guerillas or both.

In retrospect, since events went smoothly, it is easy to forget the extraordinary political risk involved. David Owen, as Foreign Secretary, had once tried to get a Labour Cabinet to agree to commit British troops to Rhodesia as part of a settlement plan. Led by Denis Healey, the opposition inside the Callaghan Cabinet had been instant and immovable. The idea of risking British troops being dragged into a Central African civil war was for them just 'not on'.

The inspired choice of Lord Soames as Britain's last pro-consul was made, in the words of one of those involved, because he was 'large, noisy and impossible to ignore'. But sending him out to Salisbury, in order to maintain the momentum of Lancaster House, even before the ceasefire agreements had been reached or his authority to act established, was a further brave gamble.

Throughout, the Prime Minister was determined to see that Lord Carrington got full credit for the Rhodesia achievement. Perhaps, in view of her known past views on the subject, she preferred not to be too publicly associated with the outcome. Although she attended the final signing ceremony at Lancaster House on 21 December, she conspicuously took a back seat, allowing her Foreign Secretary to take the well-deserved limelight. In some ways Margaret Thatcher and Rhodesia had proved to be the making of Lord Carrington. During the year he had become steadily a more substantial and serious figure. He had largely lost what one colleague called 'that giggly quality' that had previously marked his political utterances. Mrs Thatcher's personal contribution to the Rhodesia settlement, however, has for the most part been underestimated.

Rhodesia also transformed President Carter's view of Mrs Thatcher. At the outset, the Americans were frankly incredulous that any British government could produce a solution to such an insoluble African problem. The whole future of Southern Africa and Soviet-American power politics in the area rode on the outcome. As Mrs Thatcher's first year wore on, the Carter administration developed increasing admiration for her. It was reinforced by Mrs Thatcher's robust public support for American policy over issues like Iran, Afghanistan, the boycott of the Moscow Olympics, or the need for European countries within NATO to increase defence spending.

The change was dramatic, for Mrs Thatcher's election victory had filled President Carter with dismay. He had developed a close working and personal relationship over two years with Jim Callaghan and actively hoped that he would be re-elected. Callaghan had to tell him after the election that he was over-reacting and that he was sure that the President would get on perfectly well with Margaret Thatcher. His judgment proved correct. The Americans liked her brand of self-confident, pro-American leadership, so conspicuously absent elsewhere in Europe.

Ironically, Mrs Thatcher's relations with European leaders went through precisely the reverse process during the year. Both Chancellor Schmidt of West Germany and President Giscard of France took to her immediately. On 4 July, Schmidt told the German parliament that he had been 'particularly impressed by the knowledge, authority and sense of responsibility' displayed by Mrs Thatcher at her first EEC heads of government meeting in Strasbourg and at the Tokyo summit in June. Giscard, in particular, found her to be a confident right-wing political leader after his own heart when she came on her first visit, a month after the election. He was pleased by her evident and public admiration for the French nuclear power programme.

By the time the EEC heads of government met in Dublin in November, these views had been reversed. She had managed to achieve that nightmare of British European policy, simultaneously poor relations with France and Germany. In large measure it was Mrs Thatcher's close sympathy and identification with American policy that disturbed them. She evidently attached greater importance to the Atlantic Alliance with the United States than to the evolution of the EEC as a world force. French policy since the war has always had an anti-American tinge. Schmidt had never concealed his low opinion of recent American leadership of the west and thought that Carter failed to understand the importance of détente with the Soviet Union for a country in Germany's position. Neither, therefore, liked the hawkish attitudes displayed by Margaret Thatcher towards the Soviet Union in support of the United States. They were also distrustful of Mrs Thatcher's attitudes towards the very working of the Community. The whole operation of the EEC involved central intervention in policies and armies of expensive civil servants, anathema to the British Prime Minister. Influenced by chauvinist journalists like Patrick Cosgrave of the *Spectator*, Mrs Thatcher had developed very nationalistic views about the EEC, of a sort that the late President de Gaulle would have understood.

The main problem, however, was Britain and the EEC budget. Mrs Thatcher began as she intended to carry on. Within a week of becoming Prime Minister, she said in a speech, 'It has been suggested that I and my government will be a "soft touch" in the Community... We shall judge what British interests are, and we shall be resolute in defending them.' In the course of the year it became clear that her definition of British interests did not include providing our European partners with North Sea oil at below OPEC prices in the interests of a common energy policy; nor linking the pound to their European Monetary System, in the interests of a common monetary policy; nor opening our fishing grounds to their fleets, in the interests of a common fishing policy.

The budget problem in a nutshell was that in 1980 Britain, one of the poorest EEC members, was likely, because of the way the rules were drawn up, to pay over £1,000 million more to the Community than the Community spent in Britain. Mrs Thatcher thought that the other EEC heads of government could be in no doubt of her seriousness on the issue. At her first meeting with them at Strasbourg in June, they agreed to put the matter on the Community's active agenda. In her speech to the Tory party conference in October, she stressed that she and her colleagues expected 'to make very real progress at the next European Council at the end of November'. Later that month, in order to make quite certain that the message had been communicated, she added a whole section on budgetary problems to an otherwise rather high-toned speech in Strasbourg on the subject of 'The Obligations of Liberty'. Here she said, 'I must be absolutely clear about this. Britain cannot accept the present situation on the budget. It is demonstrably unjust. It is politically indefensible: I cannot play Sister Bountiful to the Community while my own electorate are being asked to forego improvements in the fields of health, education, welfare and the rest.'

Some of Mrs Thatcher's colleagues were worried at the extent to which she had the bit between her teeth on this issue. These included the majority of those on the Cabinet's defence and overseas policy committee. Howe and Nott supported her line, but Carrington, Gilmour, Pym and Walker had reservations. It was certainly inflaming anti-EEC feeling in the country. And they did not like her increasingly implied threat that the United Kingdom might be forced into breaking the EEC rules if it did not get its way.

In part this attitude reflected the consistent pro-EEC bias over the years in the Foreign Office. In part it was a strong feeling that, in the face of globally important events like Iran and Afghanistan, Europe should not be tearing itself to bits over relatively picayune domestic problems.

Lord Carrington in particular tended to this view, though his dominant preoccupation was still with Lancaster House. He expressed it at an informal pre-lunch meeting over drinks with officers of the 1922 Committee's foreign affairs group on the Tuesday before the Dublin summit. At one end of the room Mrs Thatcher was saying, 'It's such a pity Peter's so busy he can't come to Dublin.' At the other end, Carrington was saying at the same moment, 'It's a pity, but I shall have to take time off and go to Dublin to see that the whole thing doesn't get entirely out of control.' Later that week in Brussels he tried hard to play down talk of crisis and confrontation. Britain's budgetary complaint was legitimate, he said, but these questions were 'no more than family squabbles'.

If the events that then took place in Dublin Castle could still be called a family squabble, it was some family and some squabble. The other major EEC countries have become increasingly fed up at what seems to them to be perpetual British whining about poverty. North Sea oil and huge coal reserves make Britain the only EEC country self-sufficient in energy and immune from OPEC price rises. Whenever continentals come to London, the place seems prosperous enough and the streets ever fuller of Rolls-Royces. Nevertheless the other leaders had accepted the previous June that a budget problem existed. A large part of the EEC's income comes from levies and tariffs on the import of foods and industrial goods from outside the Community. As the United Kingdom has a much more open pattern of international trade than other EEC countries, the rules mean that Britain's payments to the EEC are out of all proportion to the size of its economy. The other EEC heads of government were quite prepared to enter into a conventional EEC bargain, if possible throwing other issues like energy and fishing into the package. France and Germany had let it be known in advance that they would support a scheme for a £350 million 'rebate' on the British contribution.

Margaret Thatcher, despite all available diplomatic advice,

decided to play the Dublin hand her way. She insisted that she was not asking for a penny piece of help from the Community. All she wanted was 'Britain's own money back'. Either by decreasing British payments to the EEC, or by increasing EEC spending in Britain, she wanted to see the forecast net deficit of over £1,000 million turned into 'a broad balance'. She wanted decisions to be taken at Dublin itself. The measures would have to be effective in the coming financial year. She wanted the whole loaf, or no loaf at all. She said that this must be dealt with on its merits and refused to link it with any other Community issue.

For the whole of the first day Mrs Thatcher stuck to her guns. Jack Lynch, the former Irish Prime Minister, who was in the chair, later described her performance thus: 'She certainly was adamant, persistent and, may I say, repetitive.' She succeeded in uniting the entire Common Market against her. While the others were prepared to look for compromise solutions, Mrs Thatcher's claim that Britain's contributions to the EEC in some sense still belonged to it was unacceptable. It undermined the whole notion that the Community should have its own financial resources to spend on commonly agreed programmes. The very idea struck at the heart of the EEC.

So Dublin broke up in deadlock and bad temper. Schmidt had ostentatiously fallen asleep at one moment when Margaret Thatcher was in full spate. He then told her that, if she wanted a real crisis in the Community, 'you can have it here and now'. The compromise, if it deserved that name, was that the Italian Prime Minister, chairman of the council by rotation from January, would attempt to find a way forward to a special council meeting early in the New Year. In return, Mrs Thatcher reluctantly and under pressure agreed to come to such a summit in 'a spirit of compromise', though stressing that she had 'very little room for manoeuvre'. As he left Dublin Castle, an obviously furious Chancellor Schmidt refused to answer questions from journalists, spitting out in English the words, 'I'm already deeply behind my schedule.'

The conventional view of Dublin, much put about by the Foreign Office and by detractors like Edward Heath, was that Mrs Thatcher had demonstrated her ignorance of how to do things. There were other ways to achieve the same ends, which would not have forced the other heads of government to resist as a matter of principle. Perhaps her secret ambition was to break up, or break out of, the Community itself. She had, as predicted, got herself into the fatal negotiating trap of having no politically respectable fall-back position.

At the very least, Mrs Thatcher certainly appeared to lose substantial face as a result of the Dublin summit. She herself ruefully remarked at a press conference, after being told in January by the Italian Prime Minister Cossiga that he had found it impossible to arrange an early summit, 'Patience is not one of my most obvious characteristics, but I am trying hard to learn it now.'

There is, however, another interpretation of Mrs Thatcher's tactics. She believes that major shifts in attitudes often cannot be achieved by compromise and polite negotiation. There are, in her view, occasions when the only way to shift a road block is to run a bulldozer at it. In negotiating terms, she believes that, even if there is no agreement after the blazing row at the first session, the whole argument at the second session often begins at a different and much improved level.

This at least is what Margaret Thatcher told the Tory foreign affairs group on the previous Tuesday morning that she was going to Dublin to do. She said that she knew she would not get what she wanted at Dublin. Her aim, she explained, was to 'put them on the spot' over our £1,000 million deficit. She certainly had no intention of leaving the Common Market. And the Common Market had no way of throwing us out. What was more, if we stopped paying our contributions to the Community, the remaining members would have to make up the differences themselves, which would hurt them and not us. Her conclusion, therefore, was that in the end our EEC partners would recognise that they had no option but to do a reasonable deal with us.

At this stage Mrs Thatcher assumed that the deal would be done in time for the figures to be included in the Chancellor's budget for 1980. This was not to be. Even the regular EEC summit meeting, scheduled to be held in Brussels at the end of March, was postponed, ostensibly because of an Italian government crisis. The postponement allowed Chancellor Schmidt more time for the negotiations towards an acceptable compromise that he had started in February. As the end of Mrs Thatcher's first year approached, it seemed increasingly certain that her tactics had succeeded.

Chapter 6 | *Practical politics*

As Prime Minister I couldn't waste time having any internal arguments.

Mrs Thatcher interviewed in the Observer, *25 February, 1979.*

Am I, who carry the main responsibility, not only to those who voted for us but to those who did not, living up to the convictions of a lifetime? Are those convictions standing up in practice?

Mrs Thatcher in a party political broadcast, 12 March, 1980.

MARGARET THATCHER WAS INTERVIEWED BY Kenneth Harris for the *Observer* less than three months before she found herself Prime Minister. She told him that her Cabinet would be made up solely of people who agreed with her instinctive view of the required policies, because that was the only way to get things done. It would be wrong to have a Cabinet made up of 'people who represent all the different viewpoints within the party'. In the event, despite the consistent loyalty of her deputy, Willie Whitelaw, Mrs Thatcher presided in her first year over one of the least united Conservative Cabinets in modern times. The divisions were partly concealed because until the New Year Mrs Thatcher prevented her Cabinet from having any general debate on the central issue, namely the whole thrust of the government's radically new economic policy. This remained effectively in the hands of herself and the group of like-minded colleagues who had been closest to her in Opposition, Keith Joseph, Geoffrey Howe, John Biffen and John Nott. Within the Cabinet and Cabinet Office committee structure, care for the government's medium- and long-term strategy had been placed in the hands of a small new subcommittee, consisting of Howe, Joseph, Heseltine and two officials, Sir Kenneth Berrill (head of the 'think tank') and John Hoskyns (her special adviser).

It was not until late January and February that the first major crisis of confidence in her leadership developed. The deep divisions within the Cabinet were then exposed by the combined consequences of the steel strike, the Employment Bill, the new public expenditure cuts and the second budget.

Until that point Mrs Thatcher's first year had been something of a political honeymoon. Certainly, Conservative MPs found her style as Prime Minister markedly different from Heath's and, for most, more to their liking. Heath had always managed to give the impression that all organs of the party had one function only, which was to serve his leadership. Margaret Thatcher, by contrast, knew that her relationship with and authority over the party was brittle. She had only become Prime Minister because Heath's obstinate refusal to make way after the second 1974 election defeat prevented Willie Whitelaw or any of his other senior lieutenants from getting their own leadership campaigns off the ground in time. Throughout her four years as Leader of the Opposition, she was consistently and substantially less popular in the opinion polls than the Conservative party itself. She knew the common view that if the party lost the election it would consider her a liability and unceremoniously dump her. For these reasons and because of her natural inclinations, Margaret Thatcher proved unusually attentive to back-benchers. Waiting to vote in the division lobby, for example, she mixes with the troops, knows individual names, refers correctly to individual preoccupations. Most busy Prime Ministers in those circumstances have tended to stand aloof to one side with senior colleagues. If anything, her open willingness to listen to her MPs caused her problems in her first year, because individual members, certain that they had convinced Margaret Thatcher of the vital importance of one of their pet schemes, became disappointed when nothing was done about it.

The officers of the 1922 Committee also found that their regular meetings with her, in contrast to those with Heath, had the feeling of real dialogues. It was flattering to come away with the impression that a suggestion made in a constructive spirit would result in something being done. Her performances in the House itself steadily grew in confidence during the year. As Leader of the Opposition they had been very varied. Both before and after she became Prime Minister, she took infinitely greater trouble over her set speeches than most senior politicians, writing an unusual proportion herself, chiselling away at words and phrases for hours. But she is not at all a natural orator. All the voices with which in sequence she has trained herself to speak have grated on the ears of the House of Commons. And she is not naturally good at the impromptu, often decidedly schoolboyish, exchanges which are part of the process of being a good House of Commons performer. Gradually, however, during her first year in office, Mrs Thatcher came to dominate the House of Commons. Even her warmest supporters have expressed surprise at this unexpected aspect of her transformation to Prime Minister.

Mrs Thatcher has also won loyalty by her extreme punctiliousness. She has certainly been abrasive in arguments about policy. But this has not been in any way mirrored in her personal relationships with advisers or subordinates. She writes personal notes of thanks in profusion. By Saturday, the day after she became Prime Minister, all those who had worked with her during the election campaign had received a personal note of thanks. She is notably good at keeping to her own time-table. She does not make people wait. If her demands keep a private secretary working late, she personally arranges the thoughtful snack.

Given this useful sensitivity to those around her and to back-bench MPs, it is all the more surprising that her first major political rebellion was over the question of MPs' pay. Raising MPs' salaries is always a difficult political problem, for in effect the House of Commons is voting more money for itself. Often the government of the day (and the MPs themselves) feel that circumstances require the House to set an example and accept reduced or postponed awards. The result had been a steady erosion of the real value of an MP's salary. By 1970, allowing for inflation, it was down to half what it had been worth in real terms in 1964.

In an unusual display of cross-party solidarity, the officers of the Parliamentary Labour Party and the Conservative 1922 Committee agreed on a joint policy of supporting the full implementation of the salary increase recommended by the Boyle committee on higher salaries in the public sector. Within the Tory party the Whips took the usual soundings and were left in no doubt that Tory MPs thought that the whole award should be granted on the due date. Despite this, Mrs Thatcher pushed through the Cabinet a decision that to set an example MPs should not get their full rise to £12,000 at once, but in three stages.

When Norman St John-Stevas announced this to the House on 21 June, there was an instant explosion. He got unmistakably hostile jeering from his own supporters, who had decided to make it clear to the government that it was not just dealing with Opposition back-benchers on this issue. St John-Stevas got an even rougher ride when he attempted to explain the government's decision at a meeting of the 1922 Committee. New MPs in particular were especially hostile. Much was made of the fact that someone like Harry Greenway, the new Tory member for North Ealing in London, had already taken a drop of some £3,500 a year in salary on ceasing to be the deputy head master of a comprehensive school; that MPs were now getting paid less than, say, deputy directors of local authority service depart-ments. St John-Stevas, whose heart was clearly not in the government's decision, was visibly surprised by the strength of the reaction. Nevertheless Mrs Thatcher refused to budge until it became clear that she was likely to be beaten by the votes of a Tory-Labour back-bench alliance. The government put forward the compromise that gave them their full award over a shorter period than originally proposed. As a result, the revolt collapsed.

Mrs Thatcher's handling of this episode greatly annoyed senior members of the 1922 Committee. They thought they had gone to considerable trouble to clear a path for her in advance through this admittedly tricky minefield. It also throws light on her own experience. Although Mrs Thatcher likes to present herself as an ordinary self-made woman, who knows what it is to do the local supermarket shopping, the fact is that in 1951 she had married at the age of 25 the managing director of a family paint firm, which by stages became part of Burmah Oil, leaving the original shareholders more than comfortably off. She had never, therefore, known what it was like to be the main or only salary earner in a middle class, professional family, particularly at a time of high inflation. It was for her a curious blind spot, reinforced perhaps because the first difficult executive job that she had ever done in her life was being Prime Minister.

If, apart from the question of pay, Tory MPs found Mrs Thatcher easier to get on with than any recent leader of the party, the same was not entirely true of her Cabinet colleagues. Her manner towards them was often that of a bossy, hen-pecking wife, or of a school-marm towards her intelligent, but potentially delinquent charges. The TUC leaders had noted with surprise the way in which, for example, she had treated Howe and Prior after the disastrous June meeting had broken up in premature confusion. As the Prime Minister swept out of the room, her colleagues had advanced round the table to express concern at the way the meeting had gone wrong. Mrs Thatcher came briskly back into the room and called, 'Come along, Geoffrey. Come along, Jim.' They duly followed her out of the room at once.

Cabinet ministers were also never quite sure where they stood with her much of the time. On the one hand she was a delegator. She took the attitude that she had given her ministers jobs to do and they should get on with them. She certainly did not want them to come bleating to her every time they had a problem. She did not want Cabinet agendas cluttered with indecisive papers from ministers saying that they thought the right answer to a problem was x, but that the Cabinet as a whole might have reservations and prefer y. She only wanted disputed matters, or those with a really sensitive political content, to come to Cabinet. (Even the decision in July to raise NHS prescription charges to 70p from April 1980, and thereafter to put them up in line with the rate of inflation, was not discussed in Cabinet. It was a bi-lateral concession made by Patrick Jenkin to the Treasury as a way of financing other increases in his budget and was simply reported to the Cabinet as an item in an appendix of agreed measures.) The result was that Cabinet meetings were businesslike, the agendas uncommonly short. Until the events of January and February, Margaret Thatcher seldom had more than one regular Thursday morning Cabinet meeting in any week.

She also adopted a procedure whereby ministers who could not agree could put their respective cases to her in writing, even on quite trivial matters. They would get back some note from a private secretary such as, 'The Prime Minister is clear that y is the right answer.' Y would from that moment have the absolute force of law so far as Whitehall was concerned.

On the other hand, Mrs Thatcher could not bring herself to be a delegator in the full sense of the word. In areas that interest her she always immerses herself in the greatest detail. She has a prodigious capacity for paperwork and mastering briefs. Throughout her first year, as a result, she was much given to Ayatollah-like pronouncements from on high, which wrong-footed departmental ministers and others, often in public. She combined this with something approaching an obsession with even the fine print of the manifesto on which she had been elected. Thus, although ministers were unusually free to speak and act in their respective spheres, they soon realised that this freedom was combined with a high risk of being contradicted by the Prime Minister. Her close friend and adviser on economics, Professor Douglas Hague from Manchester, found himself repudiated when he suggested that, as high tax rates came down, tax relief on house mortgages should be phased out. Even John Biffen, one of her closest Cabinet colleagues, had to accept a stinging public rebuke in January, when he suggested that the government was looking at the possibility of raising money for the Health Service by charging for doctors' visits to the home and for the 'hotel' element of stay in hospitals. She had said in the election campaign that there would not be any such charges and, even if ministers were now having to look at policies that had previously been judged politically impossible, that was not to be one of them.

Things were made harder by the fact that these prime ministerial interventions were often quite inconsistent with Mrs Thatcher's own declared general public philosophy. Charging for services was central to her idea of making the Welfare State more responsive to market forces. Yet, as a politician, she ruled out more NHS charges, or charges for nursery school places. She believed in market forces, but tried to hold down mortgage rates artificially and succeeded in preventing gas price rises in 1979. She ruled out the possibility of doing away with the special income tax allowance for the blind, an administratively cumbersome device for helping a small minority who could equally be assisted in other ways, for fear of the public reaction. For the same reason she rejected an idea from Sir Derek Rayner's efficiency unit that 300 civil servants could be saved by making teachers' pensions non-contributory, thus dispensing with the need to have machinery to collect their contributions.

The most notorious public episode of embarrassing a minister concerned Jim Prior, ironically not over trade unions, but over the steel strike. On 18 February, Prior was the guest at lunch of a group of Fleet Street labour correspondents. The basis for such encounters usually apes what is known as 'lobby rules'. The apex of the 'lobby' system is an arrangement whereby at about 4.15 pm every Thursday when the House of Commons is sitting the Leader of the House (sometimes accompanied by other ministers with topical concerns) makes statements and answers questions about current government thinking. Not only may the source of the information there provided not be revealed, but the fiction is maintained that these meetings never take place at all. It is a pernicious system of news management, but one of such convenience to politicians and political corres-ponents alike that its continued existence is assured. These 'lobby' conventions are then applied to a whole host of other exchanges between journalists and ministers. Prior assumed that his lunch at the Ivanhoe Hotel was so protected.

At some stage before lunch, in reply to a question, Prior indicated that the government did not think that Sir Charles Villiers, chairman of the British Steel Corporation, or his management, had handled the steel strike all that well. Villiers was due to retire in the summer. The Department of Industry was looking for a replace-ment, possibly an American, and the BSC would probably have to be restructured after the strike. It might be a way out of the strike deadlock if Villiers were to retire a few months early so that everyone could make a clean start.

There was nothing very surprising in Prior's comments. They accurately reflected the view of the Prime Minister and most of her colleagues. The next morning, however, national newspapers featured prominent stories, quoting Cabinet sources, that Villiers was likely to be retired prematurely. The coverage made it clear that Prior was the source. That afternoon in the House of Commons Mrs Thatcher was forced to stand up and say that she had complete confidence in Villiers and that there was no question of undermining his authority as chairman of the BSC. Then, in her *Panorama* interview on 25 February, Mrs Thatcher, who is unusually careful about preparing for such occasions and who must have expected some such question, made an uncharacteristic mistake on being asked by Robin Day why she had not dismissed or carpeted Jim Prior. She said, 'Good heavens, if you're going to kick up a terrible fuss over one mistake it doesn't really seem to be fair, does it? We all make mistakes now and then. I think it was a mistake and Jim Prior was very, very sorry indeed for it; very apologetic. But you *don't* just sack a chap for one mistake.' Prior was angered by these remarks.

Not only had he not made a mistake, he was also not apologetic. He had told Mrs Thatcher, through Ian Gow, as her Parliamentary Private Secretary, that he was sorry for the embarrassment caused by the way in which his remarks had been presented in the newspapers. He might have expected a rebuke from her in private. But as long as he was still a member of her Cabinet, she should have side-stepped the question, said that there was no question of dismissing either Prior, or Villiers, and passed on. Deliberate public humiliation of colleagues is not the way things have been done in past Tory governments.

The Prior episode on *Panorama* brought out the difference that being a woman has made to Mrs Thatcher's position as Prime Minister. She and most of her closer political friends are aware and surprised at how much this stood out during her first year. The difference is not quite what might have been expected. In projecting her personal and political image to the public, Margaret Thatcher has certainly played the 'mother and housewife' card for all it is worth, evoking response and sympathy from other women. Many women, too, have envied the way in which her appearance, clothes, grooming, hair are always just right, if in a conventional and almost classless style. But she does not have that extra dimension, obvious example in people like Barbara Castle or Shirley Williams as ministers, of being a warm personality in an essentially male environment.

On the other hand, Mrs Thatcher has not yet established a conventional Prime Minister's authority over her party. It is not that her party fails to show her respect, quite the reverse. For example, when she comes to the 1922 Committee, the Tory back-benchers rise to their feet as she enters the room, a mark of respect that they have never in the past paid to any Prime Minister or any female colleague. The same now happens when the Prime Minister joins a table for a meal in the Members' dining room. These little acts symbolise the conventional deference that Mrs Thatcher has had from her colleagues, almost all of whom are men. She has understood its worth. In her years as Leader of the Opposition and in her first year as Prime Minister this may have helped her considerably. As she has told close political friends, however, she is not inclined to think that this will work for ever in her favour, particularly if things start going wrong again. The obverse of this conventional deference is that Mrs

Thatcher finds it difficult to call upon the other semi-military code of convention, conduct and discipline which the Tory party in the past has instinctively accepted as a way in which the Leader maintains authority. She has instead a capacity for being extremely and gratuitously offensive to people in circumstances where they might otherwise be open to persuasion. As the *Panorama* episode showed, the tone of her attempts to assert authority could often sound both nagging and querulous.

The task of preserving discipline is in any case getting progressively harder for any leader. Over the years, the proportion of younger Tory MPs who are full-time politicians, unwilling to accept that their main role is confined to being fodder for division lobbies, has risen steadily. The long period of minority government from 1974 to 1979, with the government of the day regularly being beaten on important issues, fed back-benchers' sense of their own importance. The very size of the Thatcher government's majority and the fact that the Opposition itself during 1979 was in a state of almost total disarray substantially reduced the pressures for internal Tory discipline. The result was that Mrs Thatcher's first year was marked, for a Tory government, by an unusual number of revolts by groups of back-benchers against the Whips. Within a matter of weeks a small group, led by Sir Bernard Braine, voted against the terms being offered to the Barnaban islanders as part of the arrangements for giving independence to the Gilbert Islands. Throughout the summer there were serious rumblings from both right- and left-wing factions over Rhodesia.

There followed in November a potentially serious revolt on the question of immigration. Led by Nigel Fisher, the group of rebels at one stage numbered about 50 back-bench MPs, including eight Parliamentary Private Secretaries, expressing concern at the Home Secretary's proposed changes to the immigration rules. The number that would have been prepared to translate attending a protest meeting into actually voting against the government would certainly have been smaller: perhaps ten voting and a further ten abstaining, for the potential rebels were subjected to very heavy pressures by the Whips.

The manifesto had offered a three-pronged immigration policy: a new British Nationality Act to re-define who had rights to British citizenship and residence, a register of all Commonwealth wives and children entitled to settle in Britain under the 1971 Immigration Act, and a quota system to control the rate of immigration. In addition, in everything she said during the election campaign, Mrs Thatcher gave the strong impression that a Tory government would act effectively to deal with people's persistent fears about the level of immigration. Specifically, the manifesto said that a Tory government would limit the entry of the parents, grandparents and children over 18 of those already settled here to 'a small number of urgent compassionate cases' and would stop the concession under which, since 1974, women already in Britain could bring their husbands and fiancés to join them.

Despite her personal identification with these policies, Mrs Thatcher was forced to accept, as most people already knew, that the idea of a comprehensive register of dependents eligible to come to Britain at some future date was quite unworkable. A quota could not be devised that would meet its purpose, namely the exclusion of immigrants from the Indian sub-continent, without being flagrantly racialist. And a new Nationality Act was a legal minefield that would require much careful thought. Having ruled out most of this part of the manifesto, Willie Whitelaw duly introduced new immigration rules in the autumn. His problem was that the manifesto had also contained another ringing, but contradictory declaration. It was that 'the rights of all British citizens legally settled here are equal before the law whatever their race, colour or creed.' Yet his proposals were clearly designed, at the very least, to reduce the rights of a class of female citizens in comparison with their male counterparts, because the new rules did not apply to wives and fiancées. The Chancellor's wife, Lady Howe, as a former deputy chairman of the Equal Opportunities Commission, was forced to say on television that she objected to the proposals. The proposal was even more illogical because, in response to Tory pressure, girls *born* in Britain were to be exempted from the regulations. It had been seen that, in their full form, they would stop white British girls marrying Americans or Europeans and living with their husbands in Britain.

What was inescapable was that, in their anxiety to change the rules in order to keep out a relatively small number of Asian men each year, the government were proposing to put onto the statute book a measure that was clearly both racist and sexist. The Home Secretary under pressure introduced further amendments to the rules, which lessened their scope and effectiveness, without removing any of the objections to them on the grounds of civil liberty. Lord Scarman was to say that the new rules were almost certainly in breach of the European Convention on Human Rights, where Article 14 declared that sex was an inadmissible ground for discriminatory laws. Even with the Home Secretary's concessions, at least 19 Tory members defied the whips and abstained in the November vote. More may have taken refuge in pairing arrangements to avoid being in the House. Nigel Fisher in the end voted with the government, claiming that he was putting 'loyalty before conscience' (the unmasked Soviet spy Anthony Blunt had just said that he had committed treachery because he had put conscience before loyalty). One member of the government, Cyril Townsend, Parliamentary Private Secretary to Reg Prentice at the Department of Health and Social Security, resigned as a result. It had been an uncomfortable, if not a dangerous, moment for the government. The best speech in the debate, exposing the legal and logical weakness of the government's proposals, was made by the newly elected 27-year-old member for Loughborough, Stephen Dorell. Whitelaw was heard to remark afterwards that he had 'never hated listening to a speech more in my life'.

The New Year brought other problems for those in charge of the government's business. Terence Higgins, himself an ex-Olympic athlete, and others reacted to Margaret Thatcher's quite clumsy handling of the Moscow Olympics boycott. She refused, despite advice, even to inform Sir Denis Follows, the chairman of the British Olympic Committee, in advance that the government was going to call for a boycott of Moscow and for alternative games because of events in Afghanistan. The Higgins group thought that Mrs Thatcher had put her authority behind a policy that would be unpopular and ineffective. At least 17 Tory members, ranging from Edward Heath to Hugh Fraser, abstained when the government asked the House on 17 March to support its stand.

The next day four Tory MPs, led by Sir Brandon Rhys Williams, voted with the Opposition on an amendment to the Social Security Bill to indicate to the government the strength of feeling of a much more substantial group of back-benchers about rumours, which were well founded, that the Chancellor intended to cut the real value of the child benefit allowance in his budget later in the month. And, finally, even the House of Lords turned against a Tory government. Led by an unlikely combination of Lord Butler, who had been responsible for the 1944 Education Act, and the Duke of Norfolk, representing a highly effective campaign led personally by the Archbishop of Westminster in the interests of Roman Catholic church schools, the Lords threw out a proposal that would have allowed local education authorities to save money by charging for school bus services. Taken all in all, on the experiences of her first year Mrs Thatcher had no reason to suppose that she could count on a docile Parliament for the rest of her first term in office.

In matters of policy, Rhodesia remained the most striking reversal in her thinking during her first year. But there were others of importance, for example her attitude towards the British National Oil Corporation. The assumption behind this publicly owned body, set up by the Labour government, had been that the best interests of the oil companies operating in the North Sea might not always be identical with the national interest. It had finally been started by Tony Benn when he was Minister of Energy, despite active lack of co-operation from Harold Wilson, the Prime Minister, other ministers like Harold Lever and Edmund Dell, and most of the officials in the Department of Energy, from the Permanent Secretary, Sir Jack Rampton, downwards. Even Benn had only succeeded because the government needed in a hurry a vehicle through which to finance support for the troubled Burmah Oil Company, without the whole of Burmah's massive liabilities having to be provided for as government spending.

Mrs Thatcher never liked BNOC. It offended her strong prejudice that nothing in the public sector could possibly be as commercially efficient as anything in the private sector. Further, as she was given to telling people, she knew about the subject, because her husband was in oil. (Denis Thatcher, who had gone into Burmah with his family paint business, was by the time he retired a divisional director in the group, though not with a seat on the main board.) She had never been persuaded by Lord Kearton's arguments, as chairman of BNOC, that the national interest required some check on the activities of the oil companies. So despite the fact that there was no manifesto commitment to this effect, Mrs Thatcher decided immediately on coming to office that BNOC should be sold to the major private British oil company, BP. Negotiations were accordingly put in hand. BP argued that, since there was shortly to be an oil glut, they were not prepared to pay any very fancy price.

Very rapidly, however, the new energy minister, David Howell, came to the conclusion that BNOC should not be sold off. It was clear that it would shortly be making very substantial sums of money, available directly to the taxpayer. It would make no sense to forego that massive long-term revenue for the price of a single sale in unfavourable conditions in 1979. He also came to the conclusion that BNOC was indeed a useful tool in the government's negotiations with British and foreign oil companies. He was supported by Lord Carrington, who argued that the existence of BNOC would make it easier for the government to have its own positive oil policy. Throughout 1979 and the spring of 1980, therefore, Howell fought a skilful running campaign to change the Prime Minister's mind. His first successful device was that BNOC should contribute to the first budget totals not by selling itself to BP but by arranging sufficient 'forward sales' of its own oil. As the months went by and the forecasts of BNOC's profits rose hugely, the case for keeping it wholly in government hands became progressively stronger.

Howell's eventually successful campaign to save BNOC was made more difficult, however, by Mrs Thatcher's characteristic of taking strong personal likes and dislikes to individuals and allowing them to influence her views on policies. At a lunch in the House of Lords, hosted by Lord George-Brown in November 1978, Lord Kearton had publicly called the city editor of the *Sunday Telegraph*, the late Patrick Hutber, a liar for continuing to publish a story about BNOC which he knew not to be true. Kearton had gone on to say that he was more and more impressed by the Labour government and in particular considered that Tony Benn was a good energy minister, to whom the country owed a debt of gratitude for his persistence in setting up BNOC. Even the words Tony Benn seem to have a strong effect on some people. Hutber said threateningly to Kearton at the end of the lunch that he would 'fix him' for what he had said. At the time Hutber, an ex-socialist who in middle age after a chequered career had become a standard-bearer for the beleagured middle class, was quite close to Mrs Thatcher, helping her even with some of her speeches. (Denis Thatcher went to Hutber's funeral a year later, when he died after a car crash.)

From that moment Mrs Thatcher's hostility toward BNOC increased and she never had any direct contact with Kearton again. It meant, however, that Howell could not agree to Kearton's protégé, Alastair Morton, becoming the chief executive of BNOC. It also meant that Lord Kearton could not later be offered the job of chairman of the National Nuclear Corporation, though he was the candidate of the shareholding companies involved, because it was known that Mrs Thatcher would veto the appointment.

A similar relationship affected the fate of the National Enterprise Board during 1979. The chairman of Rolls-Royce, Sir Kenneth Keith, was fighting for his position against the NEB, which was his shareholder. The NEB, under Sir Leslie Murphy, had agreed with the outgoing government that the management of Rolls-Royce had proved inadequate to its task, that the financial position of the company was deteriorating, that Keith was refusing to answer legitimate questions and that he must go. Keith, however, is the sort of animal who, when attacked, defends himself. He did not know Mrs Thatcher, but had invited onto his board Sir Frank McFadzean, who had easy access to her and to Keith Joseph, not least because of his connections with the Centre for Policy Studies. Without any discussion with the NEB, Mrs Thatcher and Keith Joseph agreed that the Rolls-Royce shareholding should be taken away from the NEB and given back to the Department of Industry. They persisted in this decision, even when the entire NEB, which included a number of distinguished industrialists, threatened to resign *en bloc*, which they did in November.

The Rolls-Royce decision was curious, however, because it flew in the face of the government's declared policy towards publicly owned industries. This was that government should have as little as possible to do with them, while imposing on them a strict discipline through tough limits on the amount of money that they were allowed to borrow from the government. Yet here Sir Keith Joseph was deliberately taking Rolls-Royce back into direct control of civil servants, answerable through himself directly to Parliament, without even the advantage of the specialised buffer that the NEB represented. Further, apart from the obvious inability of Sir Kenneth Keith to get on with the NEB, it was clear that he also expected the Department of Industry to be a less disobliging shareholder than the NEB over the question of money and control.

Mrs Thatcher admitted as much when she visited the Department of Industry in the New Year. Officials asked her how, in her view, they should discharge their responsibility to supervise the company. She replied that the job was impossible. The only thing to do was to let Rolls-Royce get on with the job. It was one of those moments when Mrs Thatcher conveyed to her audience the strong impression that she did not understand the nature of the problems involved. It is not possible for a company like Rolls-Royce to receive substantial sums of taxpayers' money, while its management remains in practice responsible to no one except itself. For more than three decades people have been wrestling with the problem of how to impose commercially sensible discipline on enterprises that in the last resort are financed by the government. Direct control by Whitehall officials has usually been regarded as one of the least satisfactory.

Although, as we have seen, 1979 contained its full share of problems, an account of the seven months from May to December would be giving a quite false impression if it suggested that Mrs Thatcher and her government were labouring at Westminster. Rather the reverse. As the New Year came, in some ways things seemed to be qoing quite well. The Prime Minister could with some credibility claim that a new spirit of realism was abroad in the country, as the message went home that the government was not going to step in to help people to find solutions that they were unable to find themselves. Much, probably premature, comfort had been drawn from a series of union votes which went against the more militant recommendations of union leaders. There were heavy clouds over the state of the economy, but they had not yet darkened the atmosphere in Parliament. There had been serious rumblings amongst MPs when the bank rate had been raised to 17 per cent in November. Was this an admission that the government had totally misjudged the nature of the problem during its first summer? Had they not been told at the beginning that the government had taken the necessary steps to get public spending and the money supply under control? What had gone wrong that it was now necessary to bring in such an obvious panic measure?

Mrs Thatcher had faced these criticisms directly by addressing the 1922 Committee on 13 December. Her speech took the form of a special pre-Christmas 'end of term report' to the party. Edward Du Cann handled the situation smoothly. Although the meeting gave the Prime Minister a slightly less rapturous reception than the careful briefing to the political correspondents afterwards suggested, the back-benchers clearly appreciated and admired the way in which she directly confronted the disquiet and criticism which many were beginning to voice. Her message was that the government would not be deflected from its chosen path. She told them that more needed to be done to cut public spending so that the government could meet its financial targets without astronomically high interest rates. The task was once again in hand. It would this time involve really difficult political choices. As they banged their desks in applause, she added tartly that she hoped that they would not later 'duck the reality' of what this policy implied. It was a direct and effective performance.

In January, however, Mrs Thatcher's authority was put to its first full test. It started inside the Cabinet and inevitably centred on the public spending cuts. These were indeed forcing ministers to face politically difficult decisions. In order to get down to the totals required, every budget had to be looked at again, even if this meant disregarding past promises. Even the defence budget, where increased spending had been given absolute priority by Mrs Thatcher, came up again for review. Over this she may have come close to losing her first minister. Francis Pym was forced to make it clear that he would resign if cuts were imposed on him. Cabinet meetings began to over-run into lunch time. For the first time those ministers who were not part of the inner Cabinet dealing with economic policy spoke directly of their severe misgivings about the direction in which they were being led.

Those present recall that the debate was very open and direct. Mrs Thatcher was left in no doubt that, for many of her senior colleagues, this was the last time that they were going to participate in an attack on government spending programmes, simply in order to meet the requirements of a particular theory which involved setting ever lower targets for the amount the public sector as a whole should be allowed to borrow, regardless of what was happening to the economy. The Cabinet meeting on 24 January was a particularly sombre gathering, devoted almost entirely to cuts in spending on Social Security, where the government was clearly proposing to go back on promises made as recently as June. The Prime Minister had by then accepted that there should be no more immediate cuts in the education budget, but the other proposed reductions in local government spending were clearly propelling the government into a direct confrontation with local authorities. The coming clash would be the more embarrassing for Michael Heseltine because the main local authority associations were Conservative controlled. Patrick Jenkin emerged from one of a series of continual meetings in that last week, saying to his officials, 'We're not out of the woods yet.' Mrs Thatcher knew that her government had been blown off course and that the next two months up to the budget would in a real sense risk breaking her government. After what had in effect been an explosive running Cabinet meeting for the whole of the last two weeks in January, on the last day of the month exhausted ministers reached the compromise package that Geoffrey Howe was able to announce in his budget speech in March.

During January these divisions were for the most part kept within the government. In February, however, the crisis of confidence in Mrs Thatcher became increasingly public. For the first time, her government appeared from the outside to be showing signs of coming apart. As often happens when such a mood takes hold, individual episodes take on unusual importance. There was considerable dismay within the Tory party at the way in which David Howell had allowed the British Gas Corporation to raise its prices despite the fact that it was making large profits. The policy itself had much in its favour and Howell was reaping the consequences of Mrs Thatcher's intervention to keep down gas prices the previous summer. Even the unhappy Patrick Jenkin ran into trouble with Tory MPs when he proposed to implement a cost-saving proposal from Sir Derek Rayner, whereby Social Security benefits would in future mainly be paid by cheque, instead of over Post Office counters. This was vigorously opposed by the National Federation of Sub-Postmasters, who argued that many village shops depended for their viability on the money that they earned providing this service through sub-post offices. All of these things contributed to a feeling that the government simply had not got its act together. Whatever its message was, it was certainly failing to get it across to the people.

This impression of disarray was heightened by some 'media events'. On 7 February, Sir Ian Gilmour delivered a speech in Cambridge entitled simply 'Conservatism'. Its timing was, perhaps, more important than its content. He did not dissociate himself from the government's policies, but he made remarks that had to be interpreted as an attack on Margaret Thatcher's economic philosophy. In the Conservative view, he said, 'economic liberalism, à la Professor Hayek' was a threat to political freedom because of its starkness and failure to create a sense of community. Monetarism alone, he said, would not work and ignored necessary political reality. His further remarks could only be taken as a direct attack on the Prime Minister's view of the role of the state in society. 'The interventionist state and the Welfare State are not going to go away. This is something . . . which I welcome. Those who believe otherwise have, in my view, fallen into the trap of ideology and dogma – which is or should be to Conservatives the unpardonable sin.' Coming from a Cabinet minister, the speech was a sensational revelation of the internal debate that had been going on during January. The split between the 'hawks' and 'wets' in the Cabinet was now clearly out in the open.

Ten days later an anonymous article appeared in the *Observer*, signed by 'A Conservative MP'. Its most damaging charge was that, with the present team manning the Treasury's rococo towers, 'we are suffering from A-level economics'. An ideology had been elevated above politics, in an almost Marxist fashion. Before long the Conservative party would have to pay the price. The steel strike should never have been allowed. At Dublin Mrs Thatcher should have behaved 'a little more like Helen of Troy and a little less like Hector'. Public spending cuts were right in principle, but the arts, rural school bus fares, the sick and the mentally handicapped were not legitimate targets. And so on in a very bouncy style. The impact of the article was somewhat reduced when Julian Critchley was forced to reveal that he was the author, for the substance of what he said was overtaken by the feeling that an anonymous article was an underhand art form. There is no doubt, however, that he was expressing the views of a substantial part of the Tory party in Parliament.

More damaging perhaps was an overt attack on the Prime Minister by Malcolm Rutherford, political editor of the *Financial Times*, on 22 February. The hurt was the more because in the past Rutherford had given the impression of being rather a Thatcher fan. Basing his argument mainly on the fact that she had failed so far to sack Jim Prior, he began by writing that she was turning out to be a weak Prime Minister, continued with the view that the government was ill organised and weakly led, and ended with the judgment that, to date, she had not proved herself either strong or consistent.

Mrs Thatcher clearly had to counter-attack. For a moment she was tempted to rely mainly on an image campaign designed by Saatchi and Saatchi, the advertising agents who had masterminded her election campaign. In the end she chose the simpler tactic of going straight to the public with a restatement of the message that she was trying to get across. She went on a tour of the West Country, her first since the election, in order to get television and local news coverage. She used every opportunity to present her new line. Its theme was to play down the high expectations that her policies would produce quick results, and to stress that the goal could only be reached by sacrifice and sustained effort over a long period. At short notice she put herself on BBC *Panorama* on 25 February. Apart from the gaffe over Prior, it was a superb performance, radiating the impression of a confident, glamorous Prime Minister, with a clear vision of where she was going. She used the Tory party political broadcast on the eve of the Southend by-election on 12 March to deliver a straight 'fire-side chat' with the same message. And she used a conference of party constituency officials at Bournemouth in March as a platform for another rousing endorsement before the cameras of her kind of Toryism.

As her first year came to an end, Mrs Thatcher had re-established her position within the government. But in doing so she had expended a substantial part of her moral capital. She had not convinced her opponents within the party and they had tasted some blood. If she ever had to face again a crisis as severe as that in the first two months of 1980, she would be greatly more experienced but she would also be doing so with her authority much weakened.

Chapter 7 | *Forward to 1984*

I'm not a *consensus* politician or a *pragmatic* politician. I'm a *conviction* politician.

Mrs Thatcher interviewed in the Observer, *25 February, 1979.*

I don't think there'll be 3 years of unparalleled austerity. There will be 3 years of realism and 3 years, 4 years, 5 years, I hope 10 years, of opportunity.

Mrs Thatcher interviewed on BBC Panorama, *25 February, 1980.*

MARGARET THATCHER IS THE FIRST British Prime Minister to have studied a physical science at university. It has probably affected her approach to politics more than she or those around her have realised. A politician, or a social scientist, an economist, a historian has a strong tendency to weave some theory of how people behave and how events relate to each other, and then to make the facts fit the theory. Someone educated in the scientific method has a quite different mental process. You start with a hypothesis. You test it by experiment. If the observed facts do not fit the original hypothesis, you try something different. The whole of her first year was marked by clear evidence of her capacity to drop a policy if it was not working and start again on the other tack. To call these changes of direction 'U-turns' would be, for Mrs Thatcher, a deliberately provocative echo of the events of the 1970 Heath government. Yet there were a significant number of them and Mrs Thatcher proved herself deft at making them, while maintaining the credibility of the government's position.

In part this was just the obverse of her inexperience in coming to office, for she has shown that she learns very fast from experience. She has also displayed a highly developed capacity to change her mind without losing political face. She has changed her mind on big issues, such as Rhodesia, immigration and the sale of BNOC. She has done so also on small issues, such as the date of the 1980 budget. Tradition required that the budget should be on a Tuesday. So Tuesday, 25 March was originally selected, in order to get it in before Easter, although it clashed with the long-arranged enthronement of the new Archbishop of Canterbury. A more experienced Prime Minister would have asked why the budget had to be on a Tuesday and would have received no very good answer. A less flexible Prime Minister, having condoned a silly mistake, would have found it difficult to decide at once to have the budget a day later.

The speed with which she used the Blunt spy affair to drop the Home Office's proposed new official secrets act was another example of her ability to shift ground quickly. The new legislation was supposed to make more liberal the unsatisfactorily vague provisions of the 1911 Official Secrets Act. But the Home Office had, deliberately or otherwise, drafted a bill that in certain important areas would have had precisely the opposite effect in practice. It would certainly have prevented the exposure of the Blunt affair if it had already been in force. Mrs Thatcher sent word to a group of MPs that they should ask her a question the following day at Question Time. Michael Neubert duly did so, to the initial discomfort of many of his own side, to find the Prime Minister announcing that the bill had simply been dropped.

Mrs Thatcher may like the image of herself as a 'conviction politician' and she certainly has strong convictions. Against that, however, she has shown skills of political flexibility that, amongst contemporary political leaders, puts her in the company of Harold Wilson in his prime and in a different league from her predecessor, Edward Heath. All the evidence of her first year suggests that in future she will also show an ability to change a policy, if she has come to the conclusion that it is not working.

In her first year Margaret Thatcher was presiding over a philosophical debate within the Conservative party that will certainly continue to dominate the remaining years up to 1984. It is between those who believe that lasting and beneficial changes in society and the economy can only be achieved by negotiation and agreement, and those who believe that the situation is so desperate and the hour so late that radical surgery is required. The Priors, Carringtons and Gilmours, holding the first view, believe themselves to be heirs of the traditional Conservative view that a Tory government should be in some sense a government of the whole nation, a tradition descended in modern times from Disraeli, through Baldwin and Churchill to recent leaders like Butler and Macmillan. This school accepts that society is made up of powerful groups and institutions, of which the trade union movement is one. The preaching of dogmas and the application of doctrines to such a society achieves no constructive result. Progress can only be made by understanding the prejudices of all these groups and reconciling their interests. Any other course simply invites further sectionalism, with the pendulum of policy swinging ever further with each change of government. This school accepts that progress by consultation can only be slow. It finds offensive the doctrine that a government with a substantial majority has a free mandate, as a result, to impose its will. It argues that legislation like the 1971 Industrial Relations Act, or measures like the proposed assisted places scheme for private schools, or budgets like the first Howe Budget, which substantially benefit under 5 per cent of the population, while leaving the rest worse off – all are policies likely to destabilise British society, rather than to promote progress.

This frankly paternalist tradition is under attack in Mrs Thatcher's government from an equally coherent school of thought. The Josephs, Notts and Howes take the view that leisurely change by consent and evolution is a luxury that Britain can no longer afford. If the rapidly accelerating decline of the British economy is to be arrested, totally new attitudes and habits are required. In certain areas of the economy, like steel or cars, the rate at which their competitive position has deteriorated in the late 1970s is so rapid and the remedies required to contain the situation so radical that progress by agreement is not possible. In particular, the trade union movement, with its profoundly conservative resistance to change, is a major impediment. The investigation of and publicity for restrictive trade union practices and the support for managerial authority in disputes are central to increasing the capacity of the economy to absorb the new working practices essential to survival. The Hoskyns policy unit in the Cabinet Office specifically identifies these tasks as being at the heart of the government's whole strategy. At the same time a new 'enterprise culture' must be encouraged, in which new and dynamic companies will be encouraged to grow out of the shadow of the declining traditional industries.

The members of this school believe that the circumstances of 1979 are a tide which, if the government manage to take it, could result in a total change in the productivity of the entire British economy. To this school, winning the 1979 election on a radical Tory platform was not a fluke, but a reflection of the fact that public attitudes were in the process of change and ripe for a strong dose of leadership in the new direction. In particular they detected a major shift in popular attitudes against trade union excesses, not least among trade unionists themselves.

How history will judge Mrs Thatcher's government will depend in large part on how the balance of argument in this debate is resolved. Her own instincts place her with the second school. She has no links with the traditionally established leadership of the Tory party. Her decision to make a full statement over the Blunt spy affair was evidence of her resolve not to be party to a 'cover-up' for an establishment of which she was not a part. Her strengths and her weaknesses derive from the fact that she is an outsider, without excessive respect for the past, or for the continuity of human institutions. It is a strength because it means that Margaret Thatcher is not inhibited from a course of action simply on the grounds that, time out of mind, it has been considered to be impossible. It is a weakness because it goes with an insufficient understanding, shared by many of the financial and industrial whizz kids who were drawn to the Tory party in the 1960s and 1970s, that institutions require some assurance of continuity if they are to develop any effective long-term purpose.

It is, of course, impossible to predict which side in this argument will come to dominate Mrs Thatcher's Cabinet in the years between 1980 and 1984. The main practical test will be over policy towards industry, where the argument that excessively rapid change causes unacceptable dislocation and the argument that *only* exceptionally rapid change can prevent an accelerating decline into not so genteel poverty is clear and simple. Within the same debate will lie the question of whether Mrs Thatcher gets her way with a further major attempt at reform of trade union legislation in 1981, or whether Jim Prior continues to be able to block provocative change. As long as Mrs Thatcher maintains anything like the present balance of her Cabinet, the inevitable conclusion is that the traditional school will continue to hold the field. It will, therefore, be particularly interesting to see whether, in the autumn before the party conference, she is capable of a re-shuffle of her Cabinet that will shift the balance of power in the direction of radical change. Such a re-shuffle was contemplated in February as part of a tactical move to regain the political initiative. It was found to be difficult then. In the autumn it may be no easier.

Beneath the main philosophical debate, Mrs Thatcher has undoubtedly succeeded in introducing a new atmosphere into the ways of government. The theme is that people should stop looking to government for solutions. At a personal level this was symbolised when she visited Milton Keynes in September. In reply to demands for nursery schooling from a group of mothers who wished to work she said firmly, 'If the mothers want to go out to work, they can always set up their own play groups.'

It took some time for it to sink in that the same attitude applied, for example, to the steel strike; that Margaret Thatcher meant what she said when, in reply to a question about why she was doing nothing to intervene in the dispute, she retorted 'The honourable gentleman cannot know about relationships between nationalised industries and Prime Ministers. In a properly run government, the matter does not come to the Prime Minister.' For weeks during the most serious industrial dispute to affect her first year, Mrs Thatcher declined to see the union leaders involved. She seemed almost to have a physical revulsion against the idea of 'beer and sandwiches in No. 10', which had become part of the ritual of major industrial crises. When she finally agreed to see them in February, Mrs Thatcher revealed her genuine lack of involvement by showing to a surprised Bill Sirs, leading the union side, that she thought the more than 50,000 redundancies being demanded by the British Steel Corporation were to be achieved in 1981, rather than by August 1980, a mere seven months off.

It seems inevitable that Mrs Thatcher's government will have further major confrontations with public sector unions. Every government, Labour and Conservative, since 1966 has been severely damaged in its closing stages by such battles. It would be surprising if Mrs Thatcher had found some magic formula for avoiding conflict in the huge areas where modern government is directly, or indirectly, the employer. With the Civil Service itself, where the government has the most direct control, it has shown marked and understandable reluctance to have any real fight, either on the question of total staff levels, or on pay. In other areas in the public sector, where pay settlements were allowed above the going target rate of 14 per cent, it was assumed that there would have to be compensating redundancies, or cuts in other parts of the particular programme involved. The Civil Service unions will be remarkably resistant to this process being applied to their members.

With public sector industry, the danger is that Mrs Thatcher and her 'hard-line' ministers will have drawn the wrong lesson from the outcome of the steel strike. They went through several moods while it was in progress. In December and January, Mrs Thatcher was unhappy and critical of the way in which the BSC had handled the negotiations, apparently having provoked even the statesman-like Bill Sirs and his most moderate union into violent industrial reaction. At this stage the Prime Minister and the Chancellor would have contemplated any reasonable compromise that could bring the damaging strike to an end. Slowly, however, as the strike drew to its conclusion in March, they came round to the view that, whatever its faults of presentation and management, the BSC was in fact fighting the very battle for a more rapid rate of industrial change that was part of their own philosophy. When the strike finally crumbled, on the basis of an arbitrated settlement that gave the workers very little more than was already on offer, there was a positive inclination to think that after all perhaps the whole thing had been a necessary, if rather too expensive, lesson for the future on public sector industrial unions.

Such a conclusion could be dangerous. For the fact is that, despite appearances, the main steel union was poorly led and in a surprisingly weak industrial position. Bill Sirs projected himself as 'the man of steel' to the considerable annoyance of the other unions involved, most of whom had a different idea about the correct tactics to adopt and felt at the end that they could have got a better deal for their members at a smaller cost. On top of that, the BSC operates in a market where there is a world glut of steel, so that the threat of permanent loss of still more jobs as a result of damage done by an even longer strike was self-evidently not a bluff. And finally, as Bill Sirs was rather surprisingly to discover since it was his own industry, the capacity of the rest of the economy to survive on existing stocks of steel, on the output of the private sector and on imports was substantial. Even after three months of the strike, shortages were confined to certain special products and to certain areas. None of these weaknesses on the union side would apply to the same extent to other possible public sector strikes, say on the railways, or in electricity supply, or water, or once again in coal mining.

Any future industrial troubles will be set against the background of the single most important issue for the years remaining before Mrs Thatcher has to face a general election: the economy. If, from the second half of 1981 onwards, the rate of price increases clearly begins to fall again rapidly and the economy to expand, Mrs Thatcher will be more or less assured of re-election. If, on the other hand, by the first half of 1981 there is no sign that this is about to happen, Mrs Thatcher will be faced with an uncomfortable political choice. Either she can continue with her present economic policies and lead her party to increasingly certain election defeat, or she can change her policies. Given the natural scientist and the politician in her, there is little doubt, having tried an experiment for two years which still appeared not to be working, which choice she would make.

The question for the immediate future is whether Margaret Thatcher understands the violence of the crisis through which the economy still has to pass, if her chosen policy is to work. There are still disturbing indications that she does not. The second Howe budget will certainly have given a further sharp twist to the coming recession. The government's medium-term projections imply a drop in the level of inflation at a far faster rate than seems likely. If inflation remains higher than expected the fall in real living standards, the level of unemployment, the rate of bankruptcies will rapidly reach a point during 1981 where even Mrs Thatcher's unusual will will be tested. What is more, the model which she has accepted requires that industry and the economy should go through a spasm in order to return to the virtuous path of expansion and stable prices. The choice is simply whether the spasm should be short or extended. Yet Mrs Thatcher appears to continue to hope that the worst is past and that somehow the transformation can be achieved without more pain and suffering.

As she will discover, this is not the case. If Hayek, Friedman and others left the Prime Minister with the hope after their seminars that the only requirement was to abolish controls and to adopt a sensible target for the rate of growth of the money supply and that, somehow, about two years later the miracle of dealing with inflation would painlessly have been worked, then they did her a serious disservice. If they failed to make it clear to her that inflation can only be exorcised by a period of real austerity, and if the present government's policy is based on that failure, then the policies being pursued deserve Denis Healey's jibe that they are just 'punk monetarism'. In March Mrs Thatcher said on television that she was afraid that some things would get worse before they got better, 'but after almost any major operation, you feel worse before you convalesce'. For most of British industry, 1980 is going to feel more like a second major operation. The surgery may or may not be technically valid. The question is whether the patient can survive it.

Margaret Thatcher will also have to set these important policy decisions inside a narrowly political frame. By January some of those near her were worried, because they detected that during her first six months she had so fallen in love with the job of being Prime Minister that she had forgotten its essential political dimension. From February onwards, she increasingly devoted time to taking the message to the people and to thinking about the presentation of what she was trying to do.

This will clearly have to remain a major preoccupation for her. As the by-elections in her first year have shown, it will not be easy. All governments tend to lose popularity in mid-term and recover as the next election approaches. On the evidence of the by-elections at Hertfordshire South-West in December and Southend East in March, support for this government has drained unusually fast. At Southend a majority of over 10,000 at the general election was reduced to one of under 500. No doubt the fact that the Tory candidate was a carpet-bagger from Scotland, Teddy Taylor, who had lost his Glasgow seat at the general election, did not help; but the result was far worse than the government expected. It was clear that many floating voters, who had chosen to vote Conservative in the general election, were already disenchanted. If these were middle salary and high wage earners, disappointed in their hope that a Thatcher government would materially increase their living standards, this is likely to become a more persistent electoral problem from 1980 onwards.

More serious, from a Tory point of view, is the clear evidence given by these by-election results of a new revival of Liberal fortunes. Liberals always tend to do better under Tory governments, as former Conservative voters who cannot bring themselves to vote Labour look towards their only alternative. The significant fact on this occasion is that, although the Liberals lost two seats at the 1979 general election, their total popular vote held up surprisingly well. They came second in almost 80 Conservative-won constituencies, in more than a quarter of which the Tory lead was less than 20 per cent, well within the range of recent electoral upsets if a bandwagon began to roll against the government. Further bad by-election results, or substantial reverses in the May 1981 local authority elections, would put real political pressure on Mrs Thatcher.

If it comes, her style of government will not make her position easier. Her personal approach to politics has a greater element of clear moral purpose than many of her predecessors'. She is, however, also a politically isolated and lonely person. The murder of Airey Neave left her without the sort of total confidant that most Prime Ministers have found they needed. She has never had her own political faction. The coalition within the Tory party that elected her Leader in 1975 was an anti-Heath coalition, not a pro-Thatcher one, and as such it subsequently dissolved. All successful politics has to be based on a large degree of coalition, and Mrs Thatcher in her second and third years will be faced with policy problems if she fails to establish sufficient unity within her party. She will need to create a coalition of her own if the Thatcher Experiment is to last.

Appendix 1 | *The main events of Mrs Thatcher's first year*

March	28	Labour government loses no-confidence vote
	30	Airey Neave murdered
April	3	Denis Healey introduces 'caretaker' budget
	11	Tory election manifesto published
	24	Bishop Abel Muzorewa becomes first black prime minister of Zimbabwe-Rhodesia
May	3	Election day
	7	Reg Prentice, ex-Labour minister, joins the government
	8	Sir Derek Rayner appointed adviser on Whitehall waste
	10	Police get 20 per cent pay rise
		Chancellor Schmidt in London for talks with Mrs Thatcher
	11	Armed services get 32 per cent pay rise
	15	Queen's Speech
	16	Lord Boyd's report on Rhodesian elections published
	28	Government decides to admit 982 Vietnamese boat people
June	1	Zimbabwe-Rhodesia achieves 'nationhood'
	4	FT ordinary share index touches peak at 558.6
	6	Prime Minister on official visit to France looks at French civil nuclear programme
	7	European parliamentary elections
	12	Budget day
	15	Airey Neave's widow made life peeress
	22	EEC summit at Strasbourg
	27	Western summit at Tokyo
July	18	Government agrees to take 10,000 refugees from Hong Kong
	19	House of Commons votes against capital punishment
		The Queen starts African tour
	26	Government to sell substantial part of BNOC
	30	Mrs Thatcher flies to Lusaka for Commonwealth Conference
	31	Nigeria nationalises BP in Nigeria
August	27	Lord Mountbatten murdered
	29	Mrs Thatcher on flying visit to South Armagh
September	10	Lancaster House talks on Rhodesia open
	14	NUM put forward 65 per cent pay claim
	18	57 'quangos' abolished
	27	Manchester Central by-election: Labour holds the seat; Tory loses deposit
October	4	Ten-week-long engineering dispute ends
	9	Tory party conference opens

	24	Exchange controls abolished
November	15	Professor Blunt named as Soviet spy
		MLR raised from 14 to 17 per cent
	20	NEB resigns
	22	15 per cent mortgage rate from January announced
	26	Mrs Thatcher announces restoration of honours for political services
December	5	Miners reject strike call
	21	Rhodesia ceasefire agreement signed
	30	Dublin EEC summit ends in deadlock
January	2	Steel strike begins
	4	£1,000 million programme to update Polaris missiles announced
	30	Italian Prime Minister tells Mrs Thatcher that special EEC summit impossible
February	21	International Olympic Committee decide that Moscow Olympics will go ahead
		South Wales miners reject strike call in support of steel workers
	28	Government has 59-vote majority in its first no-confidence motion
March	4	Lord Soames invites Robert Mugabe to form Zimbabwe government
	13	Conservatives hold Southend East with 430 majority
		Government defeated in House of Lords on school transport cuts
	17	MPs vote by 168 majority for an Olympic boycott
	18	Mrs Thatcher threatens to hold back VAT contributions to EEC
	24	March EEC summit postponed
	25	British Olympic Committee vote to send team to Moscow
	26	Budget and public spending White Paper published
April	3	Steel strike ends after 16 per cent pay offer
	18	Zimbabwe gets independence
	27-28	EEC summit in Luxembourg

Appendix 2

Mrs Thatcher's senior ministers

The Cabinet

Prime Minister and First Lord of the Treasury
Mrs Margaret Thatcher
Secretary of State for the Home Department
Mr William Whitelaw
Lord Chancellor
Lord Hailsham of St Marylebone
Secretary of State for Foreign and Commonwealth Affairs and Minister of Overseas Development
Lord Carrington
Chancellor of the Exchequer
Sir Geoffrey Howe
Secretary of State for Industry
Sir Keith Joseph
Secretary of State for Defence
Mr Francis Pym
Lord President of the Council and Leader of the House of Lords
Lord Soames
Secretary of State for Employment
Mr James Prior
Lord Privy Seal
Sir Ian Gilmour
Minister of Agriculture, Fisheries and Food
Mr Peter Walker
Secretary of State for the Environment
Mr Michael Heseltine
Secretary of State for Scotland
Mr George Younger
Secretary of State for Wales
Mr Nicholas Edwards
Secretary of State for Northern Ireland
Mr Humphrey Atkins
Secretary of State for Social Services
Mr Patrick Jenkin
Chancellor of the Duchy of Lancaster, Leader of the House of Commons and Minister for the Arts
Mr Norman St John-Stevas

Secretary of State for Trade
Mr John Nott
Secretary of State for Energy
Mr David Howell
Secretary of State for Education and Science
Mr Mark Carlisle
Chief Secretary to the Treasury
Mr John Biffen
Paymaster General
Mr Angus Maude

Ministers not in the Cabinet

Minister of Transport
Mr Norman Fowler
Parliamentary Secretary to the Treasury and Government Chief Whip in the Commons
Mr Michael Jopling
Minister of State for Consumer Affairs (at Department of Trade)
Mrs Sally Oppenheim
Minister of State for Foreign and Commonwealth Affairs
Mr Douglas Hurd
Minister of State for Foreign and Commonwealth Affairs
Mr Nicholas Ridley
Minister of State for Foreign and Commonwealth Affairs
Mr Peter Blaker
Minister of State for Foreign and Commonwealth Affairs (Overseas Development)
Mr Neil Marten
Financial Secretary to the Treasury
Mr Nigel Lawson
Minister of State, Treasury
Mr Peter Rees
Minister of State, Treasury
Lord Cockfield
Minister of State for Housing (at Department of the Environment)
Mr John Stanley
Minister of State, Civil Service Department
Mr Paul Channon
Minister of State for Local Government (at Department of the Environment)
Mr Tom King
Minister of State, Home Office
Mr Timothy Raison
Minister of State, Home Office
Mr Leon Brittan
Minister of State for Energy
Mr Hamish Gray
Minister of State for Defence
Lord Strathcona

Minister of State for Industry
Mr Adam Butler
Minister of State for Industry
Viscount Trenchard
Minister of State for Northern Ireland
Mr Michael Alison
Minister of State for Northern Ireland
Mr Hugh Rossi
Minister of State for Scotland
The Earl of Mansfield
Minister of State for Agriculture, Fisheries and Food
Earl Ferrers
Minister of State for Agriculture, Fisheries and Food
Mr Alick Buchanan-Smith
Minister of State for Trade
Mr Cecil Parkinson
Minister of State for Employment
The Earl of Gowrie
Minister of State for Health
Dr Gerard Vaughan
Minister of State for Social Security (Disabled)
Mr Reginald Prentice
Minister of State for Education and Science
Lady Young

Law Officers

Attorney General
Sir Michael Havers
Lord Advocate
Mr James Mackay
Solicitor General
Sir Ian Percival
Solicitor General for Scotland
Mr Nicholas Fairbairn

Index